When You Are Weak

When You Are Weak

How Boasting in Jesus Makes You Strong

Brian H. Cosby

WIPF & STOCK · Eugene, Oregon

WHEN YOU ARE WEAK
How Boasting in Jesus Makes You Strong

Wipf & Stock
An Imprint of Wipf and Stock Publishers
199 W. 8th Ave., Suite 3
Eugene, OR 97401
www.wipfandstock.com

ISBN 13: 978-1-62032-152-2
Manufactured in the U.S.A.

To my children,
Lydia and Garrett

Contents

Preface

THE PURPOSE OF THIS LITTLE BOOK is to focus your thoughts on the wonder and beauty of your weakness in light of God's glory and grace in the person and work of Jesus Christ. To this goal, we will explore and unpack the practical theology found in 2 Corinthians 12:7–10, where the Apostle Paul writes:

> So to keep me from being too elated by the surpassing greatness of the revelations, a thorn was given me in the flesh, a messenger of Satan to harass me, to keep me from being too elated. Three times I pleaded with the Lord about this, that it should leave me. But he said to me, "My grace is sufficient for you, for my power is made perfect in weakness." Therefore I will boast all the more gladly of my weaknesses, so that the power of Christ may rest upon me. For the sake of Christ, then, I am content with weaknesses, insults, hardships, persecutions, and calamities. For when I am weak, then I am strong.

It is my intent and goal that you will be humbled by the "thorns" God has given you, that you will rest in the grace of Christ, that you might boast in your weaknesses, and that you will live a life that exhibits divine contentment in God's sovereign mercy. To help guide you toward this end, each chapter includes a set of discussion questions for either private reflection or group study.

I am thankful to the churches that I have been serving while I wrote this book—Carriage Lane Presbyterian Church in Peachtree City, Georgia, and Wayside Presbyterian Church on Signal Mountain, Tennessee. The members in both churches have taught me a great deal about leading through brokenness and boasting in Jesus. I am especially grateful to my wife, Ashley, for her steadfast support and encouragement through the writing of the manuscript and for the folks at Wipf and Stock Publishers for their patience in receiving it.

Brian H. Cosby
Summer 2012

1

The Problem of Good

I'VE NEVER BEEN VERY GOOD AT ANYTHING—running, golf, swimming, stretching. Especially stretching. For years, creating socially awkward moments became my undesired hobby. Mirrors magically reduced the size of my muscles and my basketball dreams didn't quite reach the rim. Not only did I never acquire adequate nun-chuck skills to defend myself, or the handyman knowledge of my next-door neighbor, I always seemed to lack the personal charm of Brad Pitt or the ruggedness of Clint Eastwood.

But this is life. It's a mixture of love, fear, strengths, weaknesses, afflictions, and occasional surprises—all packed into a body that strives to glorify God and enjoy him forever. This same God has endowed you, as a believer in Jesus, with certain gifts and talents to be used to honor and glorify him and to build up the body of Christ. So what are your gifts and talents? Do you feel that you are particularly *good* at something?

The Struggle to Compete

It's hard to compete with the Apostle Paul. He traveled across the Mediterranean world planting churches, was three times beaten with rods for the sake of the gospel, wrote a majority of the letters of the New Testament, and even met Jesus on the road to Damascus. A church planter, pastor, preacher, apologist, and chosen apostle of Jesus Christ, Paul had quite the resume! Even before he became a Christian, he was a "Hebrew of Hebrews," religiously following all of the Old Testament laws to such an extent that he counted himself "blameless" (Phil 3:6).

It's not hard to see why Paul would be tempted with spiritual pride. We today get puffed up over looks and muscles, church sizes and budgets. Paul, on the other hand, was used to write the very word of God!

In 2 Corinthians 12, the apostle outlines his personal struggle with pride—an inside peek into Paul's heart and temptation. Because of the revelations that he had received from the eternal God of the universe, Paul was tempted to think that somehow *he* was extra special, in and of himself. Who wouldn't? He was tempted to win the applause of men by boasting in his "special" status as God's chosen apostle.

Several years ago, I traveled to London, England, to take some classes through Samford University and to work for a human rights organization—Christian Solidarity Worldwide (CSW). Each day, I would take a train from London down past Wimbledon, about an hour-long trip. For the first few weeks, I spent my time gazing out the window at the old brick chimneys and run-down boxcars scattered across the suburban landscape. The lower suburbs of London amazed me by their structural complexity, history, and sheer expanse, despite the multi-colored graffiti sprayed everywhere.

As I glanced around the train car, my fellow passengers were all glued to their books. "Books?!" I thought to myself. "How could you read when there is so much see out the window?" The only time my traveling companions looked up was to see if their stop was approaching.

I need to point out that I was *not* a reader. I never read growing up and high school didn't exactly warm my affections for literature. But after a few weeks of working with CSW, I found myself one night scanning a row of old used books in a hole-in-the-wall bookstore. Before long, I was swept away by the stories of war and the promises of love. From Huckleberry Finn and C. S. Lewis, to George Orwell and Winston Churchill, I entered into worlds very different from my own. Reading and learning became my passion.

It wasn't long, however, that that reading and learning began to set me apart from some of my friends. I didn't originally want to be known as a smart guy, but when I got a small taste of men's praise, I wanted more.

Unconsciously, I quickly developed a competitive friendship with another guy in one of my classes. I say "competitive friendship" because we sought to out-do one another in our knowledge of things past and present, from history to politics. I spent hours pouring over the correct order of U. S. presidents, the capital cities of countries around the world, and even the latest business entrepreneurs in Great Britain. The stock market numbers became old news and we brought bigger and better nuggets of knowledge to each other's attention—especially when we were in front of our friends.

Eventually, I burned out. I couldn't keep up. It wasn't because I was tired of learning; I was tired of *competing*.

Healthy and Unhealthy Competition

Maybe you've experienced what I did. Maybe without realizing it, you are actually competing with those around you—be it your coworker, the pastor down the road, best friend, neighbor, or even your spouse! Competition can be very subtle. Taking care of your front yard, for example, can easily go from trying to simply maintain a respectful appearance to trying to win the "yard-of-the-century" award.

Obviously, there *is* healthy competition. I love playing soccer and will frequently hit the field with some guys in my community. When it's time to play, we play! My wife often reminds me—as I'm walking out the door—not to sacrifice my body for the game; advice I usually don't remember in the moment! We dig in our cleats, sprint after the ball, and do everything we can (legally of course) to get the ball into the goal. After it's all over, however, we grab lunch and enjoy some good fellowship. It's healthy competition.

The crucial element between healthy and unhealthy competition is the *heart motivation*. For example, imagine two fathers wanting their kids to behave in a restaurant. If you've been there, you can already see it! One dad wants his kids to behave because he doesn't want to be embarrassed and have others at neighboring tables talk about him. The other father wants his kids to behave because he wants them to show respect for those around them. Not a big deal, right?

But take it to a different level. The same scenario can play out where children go to college. The question becomes: Is going to a certain prestigious school more for the student's education or for the parent's reputation?

A young man called me not long ago with a depressed tone in his voice. "What's going on?" I asked, hoping it wasn't something *too* serious. "I've had a falling out with my best friend, Steve. Nothing actually happened," he paused, "but it seems like every time I'm around him, both of us try to one-up the other."

He went on to describe how it usually happened when they were in groups of people. After assessing his predicament, I told him that the next time he got the urge to compete with Steve, he needed to talk about his own weaknesses and affirm Steve's strengths. "Talk about my weaknesses?" he responded, obviously not thrilled with my advice. "If you build Steve up, there's no competition. No walls, no games. Just an open door to deeper friendship."

You might feel like my friend on the phone at times, asking, "Am I smarter, better looking, more popular, more adventurous?" Whenever we compare ourselves to anybody, we will inevitably have one of two feelings: pride or shame. If we feel that we are better than the other person, we will be tempted with pride. However, if we feel that we will never measure up, we will be tempted with shame. Here, I am differentiating between guilt and shame—guilt being sorry for what you've done and shame being sorry for who you are as a person. Are you plagued by either pride or shame? Maybe there is unhealthy competition.

You might be wondering at this point, "How can I begin to break free from this cycle of pride, shame, and competition?" The beauty of the gospel is that Jesus came to conquer our pride and free us from shame. He came to restore the image of God shattered by Adam and Eve in the garden by becoming the *perfect* image of the invisible God on our behalf (Col 1:15).

It is absolutely crucial to realize that God's standard for us is not to simply try our best; God's standard is absolute perfection. In his Sermon on the Mount, Jesus tells his disciples, "You therefore must be perfect, as your heavenly Father is perfect" (Matt 5:48). Since we all have sinned and fall short of the glory of God (Rom 3:23), we cannot attain this perfection on this side of heaven.

But this is the beautiful part of the gospel: Jesus came to live a life you and I should live so that *his* perfect obedience—his righteousness—is credited to your account through faith. On the basis of Jesus's substitutionary death and perfect obedience to all of God's commandments, you are declared "not guilty" before God. That is the heart of the gospel.

If your ultimate standing before God is not on the basis of works, looks, abilities, talents, or achievements, but on Jesus's perfect righteousness, you have amazing security and freedom. Jesus's righteousness removes the need to compete. Therefore, you can take comfort in knowing that when you are weak, Jesus is strong on your behalf.

Jesus Redeems Your Reputation

As we have seen, unhealthy competition has the end goal of establishing a reputation. The pursuit of reputation, however, reflects personal narcissism. Trading a pursuit for the glory and praise of God with a pursuit of reputation—whether good or bad—is neither safe nor right. Reputation is what we are known for. *What do you want to be known for?* Stop and let that question sink in for a moment. What characteristic or attribute is it that you want others to think when they see you or hear about you?

I want to be clear here. Being known for something isn't bad. But wanting to be known for something for the sake of building yourself up is. Being a loving mother, a wise businessman, a gentle grandfather, a just politician, a faithful preacher, or a smart student are wonderful callings and can certainly be honoring to God. But too often, a lack of gospel security causes us to seek a certain reputation only to be gripped by the fear of *losing* that reputation.

It's like the businessman who spends his early years in business accumulating vast amounts of wealth only to be shackled by the fear of losing it all. Like the businessman, many people spend their entire lives trying to be known for something, only to be disappointed when they attain the very reputation they've sought to establish. Ravi Zacharias once said, "The loneliest moment in life is when you have just experienced that which you thought would deliver the ultimate, and it has let you down."[1]

Jesus's disciples often felt the pressure of pursuing reputation. At one point in Jesus's ministry, he sent seventy-two of his disciples ahead of him to teach and to heal the sick. Luke tells us:

> The seventy-two returned with joy, saying, "Lord, even the demons are subject to us in your name!" And he said to them . . . "Behold, I have given you authority to tread on serpents and scorpions, and over all the power of the enemy, and nothing shall hurt you. Nevertheless, do not rejoice in this, that the spirits are subject to you, but rejoice that your names are written in heaven." (Luke 10:17–20)

Do you see what Jesus does? *He affirms their action while redeeming their reputation.* His disciples returned to Jesus feeling good about their accomplishments and wanted others to know that the demonic spirits were subject to their commands. But Jesus takes their desire for reputation and shows them that they can do *nothing* to earn the only reputation that truly matters—that their names are written in heaven!

Like the disciples, we continually seek to build up our reputation in front of others—to be known for what we can do, the people we know, or what we have accomplished. We begin rejoicing, like these disciples, over the prospect of greater popularity and recognition. But Jesus gently reminds us that *he* has become our reputation before God, and *that* is the only worthy reputation in which to rejoice. Jesus has come to redeem our reputation.

1. Zacharias, "Our Disappointments Matter to God." Adapted from a message by Zacharias based in part upon a chapter from his recent book *The Grand Weaver* (Zondervan, 2007).

Being Too Attractive

One of the things I love about my wife is that she is content to live simply. She doesn't need jewelry or expensive gifts to be happy. When we were married in Birmingham, Alabama, I was so nervous. I stood there looking at the most beautiful woman in the world in amazement that she had agreed to marry *me*! On that gorgeous spring day, we entered into a covenant together, exchanged vows, and gave each other rings as tokens of our commitment and love.

Now imagine how my wife might have felt if—when she gave me the ring—I said, "This ring is amazing! It's so shiny and round. I'm really excited to be married to you because of this ring." She would probably wonder what we were doing getting married in the first place!

A wedding ring isn't designed to bring attention to itself, nor is it designed to bring attention to the one who wears it, but to the one who *gives* it. It is meant to point to the covenant vows of the giver. In the same way, gifts and talents are not designed to bring attention to themselves, or even to the one who is gifted and talented, but to the Giver. Any elevation of gifts above the Giver is idolatry.

Because we are so prone to wander, we can actually turn our affections and worship of Christ toward someone with great talent, status, giftedness, and achievement.

If you are currently in ministry in an active church with lots of programs and exciting opportunities, be leery of the hidden hook of achievement. The spoken and written decoration on church websites, flyers, or even during Sunday morning announcements can easily become one of achievement. As I write this, there is a church down the street with a sign out front that reads, "The friendliest church in town!" Don't be so attractive in your reputation before others—accomplishments, people you know, looks, abilities, etc.—that people begin following you rather than following the Lord. While being good at something can bring glory and honor to God, as it should, being good can also be a problem.

Being With Somebody in Weakness

Can you think of a time when you have been *with* somebody in weakness? It could be a time when you came humbly and with a sense of your own brokenness to meet with and share with another in need? Or it might have been when you lead others with humility—what Dan Allender calls, "Leading with a Limp," in his 2006 book of the same title.

The Apostle Paul made a conscious effort to curb others' praises of him so that *God's* name would be renowned, not his. Put simply, Paul desired to make God famous. He wanted his readers to trust not in his own eloquence or accomplishments, but in the power of God to free people from the bondage of sin. Paul writes to the Corinthian church,

> And I was with you in weakness and in fear and much trembling, and my speech and my message were not in plausible words of wisdom, but in demonstration of the Spirit and of power, that your faith might not rest in the wisdom of men but in the power of God. (1 Cor 2:3–5)

The amazing thing about being with somebody in weakness is that it turns competition to compassion, from seeking your own reputation to God's reputation.

It is not difficult to see that rock-star preachers are on the rise, especially on television. They have more talents and gifts (and oftentimes more money!) than they know what to do with, and will promise great financial reward if you "sow the seed of faith" in their ministry. They come through the tube with "plausible words of wisdom"—seven keys to your best life now—and throngs of people sing the praises of their books, sermons, and self-help advice.

But is the *focus* on exalting the Christ who came to seek and save the lost? Are their words imbued with the truths of humanity's sin, Christ's atoning sacrifice, justification, spiritual adoption, and sanctification? Make no mistake about it: Being with somebody in weakness does not mean compromising the truths of the gospel. Actually, it means precisely the opposite. How beautiful are the feet of those who bring the good news of Jesus, bearing the *whole* counsel of God's word!

I have no idea why you picked up this book. There could be any number of reasons. But I pray that you will find in the pages that follow a freedom, intimacy, and acceptance not in self-help advice, but in the message of the gospel—*that Jesus has accomplished for you all that God requires of you so that his power might be perfected in your weakness.*

Toward a Right Use of Good

Before we conclude this chapter, I want to be clear that spiritual gifts and talents—being good at something—are desirable things and should be studied and put into practice. We are aiming for a *right* understanding of those gifts—for the building up of the church and the glory of God.

All Christians have spiritual gifts. Paul writes, "Now there are a variety of gifts, but the same Spirit, and there are varieties of service, but the same Lord; and there are varieties of activities, but is the same God who empowers them all in everyone" (1 Cor 12:4–6). As all the members of the body work together to perform a function, so also God has "arranged the members in the body, each one of them as he chose" (v. 18). Similarly, Paul writes elsewhere, "Grace was given to each one of us according to the measure of Christ's gift" (Eph 4:7).

So I ask the question introduced at the beginning of this chapter: *What are your gifts?* Here are five steps to help you think about your specific gifts and how to put those gifts into practice in your local church.

First, *identify your God-given personality*. God has endowed you with natural interests and proclivities and there are many kinds of personality tests that can help you identify those. Some of these tests include the Myers-Briggs, the DISC, and the Right Path Profiles. For example, I am a planner and I love making to-do lists and checking items off as I go. This is a personality trait and helpful to know, especially as you work with others who have varying personalities. For example, if someone persistently shows up late for meetings or has a hard time planning ahead, you will probably have greater patience knowing that such behavior is a common trait of his or her personality.

Second, *study the spiritual gifts in Scripture*. First Corinthians 12–14 and Ephesians 4 are good places to start. Grab a commentary from someone you trust and examine those texts of scripture. Do you see any of those gifts exhibited in your own life? Some of these gifts include teaching, serving, hospitality, and mercy ministry. A helpful exercise would be to write these down and ask those who know you best to tell you how they see you being used to build up the body of Christ.

Third, *ask your church's pastor or church leaders about the greatest needs of the body*. Oftentimes, you will already know some of these. But, being submissive to the church leadership will not only communicate a sense of willingness to serve, but will help the overall vision and mission of your local church.

When we joined our church, we stood before the congregation and made a public profession that we would support the peace, purity, and work of the church. I realized that this might mean not doing the things I *wanted* to do. Cutting the church's grass might not be on the top of my list, for example, but it helps create an inviting atmosphere for visitors.

Fourth, *prayerfully prepare a plan of action with specified time restrictions.* I say specified time restrictions because you will need to evaluate whether or not your gifts are adequately being used to their full potential. You might also be sensing another ministry within the body. This is usually good to do every third or sixth month.

Finally, *serve Jesus by serving the body—with gospel motivation.* Too often, serving others with your gifts means doing something good "just because we should." However, we are to reflect on the gospel—that Jesus came not to be served, but to serve and to give his life as a ransom for many (Mark 10:45).

Reflecting upon the grace of God in forgiving us, justifying us, and making us his adopted sons and daughters should lead us to serve with grateful hearts unto the Lord. And the beauty of gospel-motivated service is that God grows our faith and love for him and others *as* we are poured out.

Christ redeems the "problem of good" by becoming the *best* on your behalf. He has come to make God famous by drawing out your God-endowed gifts, for his glory and your joy. May the pages that follow give you greater clarity into how boasting in Jesus makes you strong.

Discussion Questions

- How do you want to be known? Does your life reflect that desire?

- Are there subtle ways in which you are in an unhealthy competition with those around you?

- How might boasting in weakness remove the seeds of unhealthy competition?

- What might "being with somebody in weakness" look like?

- List some of your God-given natural abilities, talents, and gifts. How might your gifts be used in the community of the local church?

2

Thorns in the Flesh

I LOVE BACKPACKING IN THE Great Smoky Mountains National Park, located along the Tennessee-North Carolina border. And I especially love backpacking in the wintertime. There's something about the cold air, the shimmering moonlight spread across the crunchy snow, and the warmth of a fire that awakens my appetite for adventure. And . . . there's no bugs!

A few winters ago, two of my friends and I hiked from the Cades Cove Campground up to Spence Field Shelter on the Appalachian Trail. The trail boasts beautiful creeks, rhododendrons, and a sweeping view of adjacent mountains and valleys. While the hike is relatively short (5.2 miles), it's straight up. It's like walking up a five-mile snowy staircase with a thirty-pound backpack!

But the reward of arriving at a rat-infested, three-sided, log shelter is totally worth it! The three of us, exhausted from the trek, brimmed with contentment. The journey forced us to grab life by the walking sticks and experience the joy of raw living.

But the best part, though, was sipping on some hot chocolate around the campfire—sharing stories of the past and dreams of the future. The fire warmed our hearts and our socks. All was going good until I had to go get firewood.

Taking my serrated saw, I marched out from the coziness of my mountain home to find branches or a fallen tree. The rule of thumb when it comes to firewood: the louder the snap the better the burn. Green or rotten wood won't work. Finally, after some exploring, I found an oak tree that had been hit by lightening and split. Though dead, it wasn't *too* dead. I began sawing and breaking off limbs until a little pile started to form.

While pulling on one particular branch, my hands slipped and a splinter shot into my palm. "Yeeouch!" I squealed, quickly glancing around to see if anybody was watching or listening. Nope. Just a few friendly owls and bears.

The splinter went in past the point of pulling it out with my fingers or a pair of tweezers. I didn't have a needle and I wasn't man enough to dig it out with my pocketknife. We still had two more days on the trail so I figured I just needed to grit my teeth and bear it.

However, every time I stuffed my sleeping bag into my stuff sack or put on gloves, I felt a sharp twinge of pain shoot up my arm. It became infected, sore, and unyielding. I couldn't escape its nagging presence.

Paul's Unyielding Splinter

In 2 Corinthians 12:7, the Apostle Paul describes the unyielding presence of a "thorn" in his flesh. The context is clear that this thorn is not a *literal* thorn, but rather a graphic symbol of some physical ailment, sin struggle, or some other personal weakness that Paul was experiencing. We know from other places in his letters that he—like you and me—struggled with sin (Rom 7:15–19; 1 Tim 1:15) and that he probably had poor eyesight (Gal 4:13–15). But the text isn't clear on the thorn's exact identity.

15

What we *do* know is that this thorn was given to Paul—by the sovereign love of God—to keep him from becoming too conceited. Literally, "puffed up." As we touched on in the last chapter, Paul is tempted with spiritual pride because he received direct revelation from God (2 Cor 12:7). God sent the apostle a thorn of weakness to keep him dependent upon divine grace.

That Paul calls this thorn "a messenger of Satan" is interesting. So, is the thorn from God or from Satan? Scripture is overwhelmingly clear that nothing happens apart from the sovereignty of God—which is displayed in both his eternal decrees and temporal providences. Wars, job promotions, relationships, and even the crucifixion of Jesus all happen according to the definite plan and foreknowledge of God (cf. Acts 2:23). Not one "maverick molecule"—as R. C. Sproul has argued—can exist apart from God's sovereign control.

At the same time, God uses people, and even Satan, to bring his eternal plans to fruition. In the story of Job, for example, Satan is presented before God and it is *God* who initiates the conversation: "Have you considered my servant Job, that there is none like him on the earth, a blameless and upright man?" (Job 1:8). Satan tells God that Job is faithful *only* because God has made him rich. Satan then asks God to tear the temporal blessings from Job. God answers, "All that he has is in your hand" (v. 12). One after one, Job's house, cattle, and family are destroyed.

The story of Job begs the question: Why suffering? But God never directly answers it. God simply communicates toward the end of the book that he alone is God and is perfectly free and just in all of his actions. God wants to show Job an aspect of his sovereign and holy character that Job has not understood or appreciated before.

Make no mistake about it: The thorns of weakness we experience *in* this life are part of God's story *for* our life—even when Satan tries to use those "thorns" for his own evil purposes. All events, all weaknesses, all injustices, and all sufferings work together for good for those who love God and are called according to his purpose (Rom 8:28). We should take up our lodgings in the perfect promises of God, that nothing can separate us from the sovereign hand of the Rock of Ages.

One final point with regards to the word "thorn." Paul employs the Greek word *skolops* for "thorn" in 2 Corinthians 12. This word was used in ancient Greek literature to describe massive spikes thrust into the outer walls of a city to protect it from invading armies. It was also used to describe tall pikes that carried the heads of fallen victims of war. The meanings associated with this word communicate that what Paul experienced was no small thing—but a visceral, deep, and heavy burden.

Do you have a *skolops* of weakness?

The Thorn of Sin

Perhaps the most obvious thorn we experience is the thorn of sin. In his book, *The Gospel-Driven Life*, Michael Horton argues that sin lies in the heart as well as in the actions that spring from the heart. He writes, "Sin is first of all a *condition* that gives rise to particular *actions*."[1] Sin affects our attitudes, desires, thoughts, and even how we view other people. But the prickles go much deeper.

When Adam and Eve disobeyed God in the garden of Eden (Gen 3), it affected all those who would come after him—it affected you and me! Adam served as our

1. Horton, *Gospel-Driven Life*, 55.

representative head, which means that the decisions he made affect those whom he represented.

I played soccer growing up and loved being the team captain. Before each game began, the referee would call the team captain from each team to the center of the field and toss a coin to see which team would start with the ball. As the team captain, I made a decision on behalf of the team that affected the course of the game. I served as my team's representative.

In the same way, Adam's decision would set the course of "team human." When God tells him, "of the tree of the knowledge of good and evil you shall not eat" (Gen 2:17), he has a free moral decision to make. If he obeys God, he will enjoy the blessings of life. But if he disobeys God, he will experience the effects of sin, misery, and death. As we learn from Genesis, the fruitful offer from Eve is irresistible and he takes a bite. After some initial blame shifting, God lays out the consequences for their disobedience, which interestingly included the presence of "thorns and thistles" (Gen 3:18) springing up as a fruit of the Fall.

Adam's sin was credited to the account of humanity and, since then, every person has been born with a natural aversion to that which is good. Our heart is like the broken wheel of a grocery store shopping cart—veering our lives into the aisles of grief, corruption, and weakness. Even when a two-year-old is told not to touch the wet paint, there is an immediate display of rebellion!

Oftentimes, if you're like me, we have a hard time even understanding the fluctuating desires and emotions of our heart. Jeremiah prophesied: "The heart is deceitful above all things, and desperately sick; who can understand it?" (Jer 17:9).

For the believer, the thorn of sin can become an *unyielding burden*. If you have ever battled a particular sin before—pride, gossip, lust, gluttony, or the like—you probably understand the feeling! It's like trying to come up for air under water without ever reaching the surface. It consumes all of your thoughts and attention while, at the same time, plunging you down by the weight of shame. Each time you sin, especially when it's against someone you love, the thorn drives deeper and deeper and you begin wondering if there's any hope.

The thorn of sin is so serious that nothing short of the grace of God can break its ugly barb and begin the process of healing. The gospel is not the good news of *sola bootstrapia*, whereby you pull yourself up out of the muck and mire of sin, but of *sola gratia*—the grace of God displayed in the accomplishment of Jesus for sinners.

How can you begin the process healing? The healing path begins by confessing sin and boasting in Jesus. James writes, "Confess your sins to one another and pray for one another, that you may be healed" (Jas 5:16). Confessing your sin takes courage and makes you vulnerable. It's an acknowledgement of weakness. But it's also an acknowledgement of your need and reliance upon divine grace. Confessing weakness drives you to the One who is strong on your behalf.

The Thorn of Suffering

In addition to the thorn of sin, there is the thorn of suffering. Suffering is not, in and of itself, evil. It is the effect of the Fall of Adam and Eve. Adam's rebellion brought a host of both external and internal sufferings into the human story—into *your* story.

Physical impairment, disease, and pain all describe elements of external suffering. As mentioned above, Paul probably struggled with poor eyesight, which no doubt caused many frustrating moments throughout his life. However, physical suffering, in itself, typically isn't as difficult to bear as internal suffering. Oftentimes, it is more difficult to bear the burden of losing a spouse or child than having an illness. Internal suffering includes shame, despair, rejection, loneliness, unrelenting fear, and depression.

The issue of suffering is also the most common argument leveled against the existence of God or, at least, some aspect of God's character. If God is good, then he isn't powerful enough to stop suffering. If God is powerful, then he isn't good enough. Maybe he is good and powerful, but he just doesn't know when suffering will come. Of course, all of these conclusions find no warrant in scripture. God's word affirms that God is completely and perfectly good, powerful, and knowledgeable—even with reference to suffering.

So why does God not only allow suffering, but also ordain it? While a thorough answer is beyond the scope and purpose of this book, let me give you three general reasons and eight specific reasons given in scripture.[2] The three *general* reasons are:

1. For the glory of God

2. For the good of God's people

3. For the judgment of the unbelieving world

Eight *specific* reasons that God ordains suffering for the believer are:

1. To reveal, deter, and mortify sin in the heart

2. To produce godliness and spiritual fruit

3. To allow the believer to experience the character of God

2. For an in-depth treatment of these, see Cosby, *Suffering and Sovereignty*.

4. To relinquish the temporal for the eternal

5. To produce a sincere faith, devoid of hypocrisy

6. To encourage fellowship with God through Word, prayer, and sacrament

7. To bear witness to the watching world

8. To cultivate communion with Christ, the greatest sufferer

Without a doubt, the American church has become directionless with regards to suffering. When tragedy strikes, we don't know where to turn or how to begin making sense of it. We don't know how to respond in God-glorifying ways nor do we think about it biblically.

When I was fourteen years old, I lost my mom to cancer. I wasn't prepared for it even though I watched her life deteriorate for years on end. All I knew to do was to bottle up my emotions, fears, and pain and try to steer clear of any conversation or event that would open it back up. Maybe you can relate.

The thorn of suffering pounds the conscience with a sense of weakness. The angry phone call telling you he's not coming back. The suicide note brimming with regret. Burying a child before her fourth birthday. All of these painful experiences stem from the thorn of sin. They remind us that sin came into this world through the Fall, as part of the curse of sin.

Sitting in jail, the Apostle Paul writes to the Philippian church that he has suffered the loss of all things, "that I may know him and the power of his resurrection, and may share his sufferings" (Phil 3:10). Paul wants to somehow share in the sufferings of Christ—to experience something of the sweet communion with his Savior. Affliction becomes the breeding ground of affection and love. James writes,

"Count it all joy, my brothers, when you meet trials of various kinds" (Jas 1:2). Could you say the same in the midst of your trials?

The beauty of the gospel is that even in the deepest possible pain, we can find rest and peace. God may not remove the actual pain, but redeems the pain for his glory and our joy. Faithful men and women in ages past would often sing praises to God while being burnt at the stake for their faith. How could this be? Because they knew that while sorrow would last for the night, their heavenly joy would come in the morning.

The thorn of suffering reminds us of our weakness and drives us to fall upon the mercy of God. It's in that moment of crying out, "I can't do this any longer on my own!" that we find healing. It's in that moment of exhaustion that we begin to learn what it means to come and find rest for our weary soul in the sufficiency of Jesus—that his yoke is easy and his burden is light. And it's in that moment of weakness that we become strong again.

Thorns of the Cross

I mentioned earlier that the word "thorn" in Greek— *skolops*—held a variety of meanings in the ancient world. But I didn't tell you that it also referred to those spikes driven through the hands and feet of those nailed to a cross. The beauty of the gospel is that the thorns of sin and suffering collided on the cross of Christ as an expression of covenantal, unfailing love. *Our thorns of sin were driven into his hands and feet so that we might experience a love that would never let us go.*

Paul writes, "For our sake [God] made him to be sin who knew no sin, so that in him we might become the righteousness of God" (2 Cor 5:21). The declaration has come to the thorn-laden sinner! "NOT GUILTY!" The second Adam—Jesus Christ—has conquered sin, death, and Satan and has inaugurated the kingdom of heaven for all who believe.

Our thorns of weakness show us that we are to be strong in Christ. He has become our righteousness, our strength, our salvation. He is the truer and better Adam, Abraham, Moses, Joshua, and David. He won the title of The Righteous One through perfect obedience and, through the joy that was set before him, endured the cross. The King would don the crown of thorns and embody strength in weakness. When you are weak, boasting in Jesus makes you strong.

Discussion Questions

- How might sin become a relentless burden and weight?

- Have you ever experienced a continual, unyielding "thorn" of suffering? See if you can identify a personal example of both external and internal suffering.

- How might the community of faith, the local church, be a part of the healing process for both thorns of sin and thorns of suffering?

- How has Jesus conquered sin, death, and Satan? How do you receive his victory?

3

Finding Freedom Through Failure

THE DENOMINATION I SERVE—the Presbyterian Church in America (PCA)—practices the (quickly) fading ordinance of church discipline. In fact, church discipline, the preaching of the Word, and the administration of the sacraments make up the "marks" of any local church. It is that important!

Over the years, I have seen many people go through the process of church discipline. The purpose of church discipline is threefold: (1) to restore the impenitent sinner, (2) to warn others of the gravity of sin, and (3) to promote the peace and purity of the church. When a church member has sinned and, when confronted, remains unrepentant and defiant, we usually begin the process of church discipline. This, to be sure, is part of a person's membership vows— "Do you submit yourself to the government and discipline of the church?"

Recently, I witnessed a middle-aged man who had committed adultery confess his sin before the church after ten years of impenitence! We experienced the beauty of the gospel and he was welcomed back into the body of the church. He experienced freedom through failure. But his freedom only came through his faith in the good news of Jesus Christ. How can you find freedom through failure?

Breaking Point

Imagine taking a dowel rod and bending it—like a rainbow—to the point of breaking. Just before it snaps, you sense the strain and pressure of the rod and it could give way at any moment. It might even begin making those first sounds of creaking and splintering. And then, in a split second, you hear a loud crack and immediately all the strain and pressure is gone and, of course, it is now broken.

Maybe you can already make the connection. Many of us live under enormous pressure and strain, never at peace and never really breaking. We try to keep up an image and perception before a watching world that we have it all together—while underneath, we are burdened by stress, guilt, and shame. Brokenness, the idea that you admit and offer up your fears and failures, can be a welcoming relief.

The Fig Leaves of Pretending and Performing

We all know the feeling of being vulnerable. After their fall into sin (Gen 3), Adam and Eve immediately became aware of how vulnerable they really where. No longer did they enjoy unhindered communion with God. Rather, they had an unyielding sense of being shamefully naked. So, they did what we all do when confronted by our sin and failure—*they covered up and hid themselves.*

Moses describes what happened. First, "they sewed fig leaves together and made themselves loincloths" (v. 7). Then, "the man and his wife hid themselves from the presence of the LORD God among the trees of the garden" (v. 8).

When we fail, our typical reaction is to cover up and hide. When we sin, our typical reaction is to either act like we didn't sin, justify our sin, or grab the nearest fig leaf of self-righteousness to cover up our sin. In other words, we *pretend* and *perform*.

In *The Gospel-Centered Life*, Bod Thune and Will Walker of World Harvest Mission clarify these two harmful realities of pretending and performing:

> Pretending minimizes sin by making ourselves out to be something we are not. Performing minimizes God's holiness by reducing his standard to something we can meet, thereby meriting his favor. Both are rooted in an inadequate view of God's holiness and our identity.[1]

Oftentimes, we pretend that we are not as bad as we really are. The truth is, however, we are more sinful than we could ever imagine. The heart is prone to wander and, as the Apostle Paul writes, "For I know that nothing good dwells in me, that is, in my flesh" (Rom 7:18). The problem of pretending is that it shackles your conscience and chains you to the wall of disharmony and inner turmoil.

I was in a Japanese play as a kid. The only thing I really remember? Wanting to be finished! While acting, I was under constant stress and pressure. The same goes for acting in the Christian life. You cannot find freedom and peace when you are pretending to be somebody you're not.

So who *are* you? While you are more sinful than you could ever imagine, you are more loved and treasured—through faith alone in Christ alone—than you could ever dream or imagine. As a justified sinner, you are an adopted child of God, whose love for you will never let you go. You have a new heart, a new allegiance, and new desire to please God. As we shall see, your unchanging position and status before God is the very key that unlocks the door of freedom and peace.

1. Thune and Walker, *Gospel-Centered Life*, 9.

Besides pretending, however, we also succumb to *performing*. Our default mode is to offer up our good works to God as if to earn his love and acceptance. The well-known stanza from "The Solid Rock" changes to "My hope is built on nothing less than my good works and righteousness."

There is only one garment that can remove the withering fig leaves of pretending and performing and secure you in a freedom inexpressible—the righteous robe of Christ's righteousness. John Stott writes, "We have to acknowledge our nakedness, see the divine substitute wearing our filthy rags instead of us, and allow him to clothe us with his own righteousness."[2] The more you lay hold of and realize your security in the merits of Christ on your behalf, the more you will experience freedom through failure.

Let's get practical. Let's say that you're a husband (ladies, this is for you too!) who doesn't provide the spiritual leadership in your home that you know you ought to provide. You feel the pressure and stress to pray or read scripture before mealtimes or when the kids go to bed, but you feel inadequate or are simply lazy. Perhaps, you've never led your family in worship, Bible reading, or other areas of spiritual leadership and it would simply be too awkward to start.

You have a decision to make. You can continue living with the constant burden of failure, stress, and pressure by pretending everything is fine. Or, you can realize that you are so completely forgiven and secure in Christ that you can admit failure and begin leading your family with the freeing grace of God.

Your family isn't looking for perfection; they are looking for repentance—a repentance rooted in the gospel of Jesus Christ.

---

2. Stott, *Cross of Christ*, 162–63.

Be aware, therefore, of your heart's tendency to fall into the peace-stealing, freedom-destroying, and joy-sapping traps of pretending and performing. They are nothing but fig leaves.

What is True Freedom?

Have you ever thought about *why* you long to experience freedom? Why is it that so many of our songs exhort us to let freedom ring? Why is it that the image seared into our brain from *Braveheart* is William Wallace yelling, "Freedom!" at the top of his lungs—even as he dies?

What is true freedom?

In and of itself, freedom is the state of being free from confinement, bondage, or restraint. It carries with it the notion of independence or autonomy. But the biblical understanding of freedom—*true* freedom—goes much deeper.

In Galatians 5:1, Paul writes, "For freedom Christ has set us free; stand firm therefore, and do not submit again to a yoke of slavery." Kaspar Olevianus, co-author of the Heidelberg Catechism (1563), commented on this verse:

> This is what it means to be set free from sin, that the curse has been lifted and our sins are not counted against us. Our freedom is given to us by the sacrifice of Christ, which retains its force in eternity and makes us sure that God will not be eternally angry with us.[3]

True freedom comes through both the actual act and experience of God forgiving all of your sin and counting you righteous in his sight through the accomplishment of Christ.

3. Quoted in Bray, *Galatians, Ephesians*, 170.

Thus, true freedom is deeply spiritual. The unbelieving heart, therefore, cannot experience true freedom. It will always seek to clothe itself with the fig leaves of self-righteousness.

Make no mistake about it: *True freedom is not independence or self-autonomy, but rather utter dependence upon divine grace.* The spirit of God replaces the heart of stone—chained to the floor of self-reliance—with a new heart of freedom and peace. Indeed, "Where the Spirit of the Lord is, there is freedom" (2 Cor 3:17).

The liberty bell of the gospel rings true in a life that's been ransomed from the bondage of sin and death through faith in the finished work of Christ. Again, John Stott explains,

> For the essence of sin is man substituting himself for God, while the essence of salvation is God substituting himself for man. Man asserts himself against God and puts himself where only God deserves to be; God sacrifices himself for man and puts himself where only man deserves to be. Man claims prerogatives which belong to God alone; God accepts penalties which belong to man alone.[4]

The Beauty of Breaking

Nobody likes being a failure, unless it is to gain attention. I remember several of my classmates in high school who seemed to take pride in failing tests. "I bet I got a worse grade than you!" As if that made sense.

But, typically, failure doesn't seem redeemable. It doesn't seem like there can be a purpose for pain. The pain

4. Stott, *Cross of Christ*, 160.

of failing—whether it be a task at your job, a grade in school, or just simply being a good friend to somebody—can weigh you down and become a driving thorn of despair. But *why* the failure; *why* the weakness? The one who seeks to understand purpose in pain only has to look so far as the cross of Jesus Christ. There, for the joy set before him, he endured the cross. The infinite love and justice of God collided and Jesus cried out, "It is finished!"

If you have put your faith and trust in the Lord Jesus Christ, your hell was fully experienced 2,000 years ago, by Another. More than that, the unyielding demands of God's holy and perfect law were equally matched by Christ's obedience, on your behalf.

The good news of the gospel is that Jesus came, not to free his people *from* their failures, but to free his people *in* their failures. The weight of your weaknesses falls by the wayside when you realize that Jesus is strong on your behalf. Or, to put it another way, Jesus's life of holiness is the springboard to your pursuit of holiness.

But note the parallel call of growing in grace: While we pursue personal holiness, we boast in weakness. And the reason that we can boast in weakness even as we pursue holiness is that our holiness is Jesus. He has become our righteousness (1 Cor 1:30). Therefore, as Paul writes, "Let the one who boasts, boast in the Lord" (v. 31). Bryan Chapell explains that, "Our holiness is not so much a matter of what we achieve as it is the grace our God provides."[5] If you are a Christian, God has already declared you holy and righteous in his sight. *The Christian life is the continual growth into that which you have already been declared.*

Do you know your areas of weakness? Have you identified your greatest worries, fears, and the times when you

5. Chapell, *Holiness By Grace*, 8.

fall into temptation the most? Do you long to be free from the burden and weight of guilt?

Please hear this loud and clear: Apart from the gospel, you will not find true freedom. I'm not just talking about becoming a Christian; I'm speaking directly to you who profess faith in Christ. The gospel doesn't just provide the doorway into the life of faith; the gospel provides the entire foundation for the ongoing life of faith.

Oftentimes, the Christian life is set before the watching world as a list of rules and laws for people to follow. If they keep the commandments and laws, they are good Christians. While Christianity certainly contains the laws and commandments of God, the essence of the Christian faith is that God has rescued a people who not only *didn't* keep his laws—they *couldn't* keep his laws! Paul writes, "For the mind that is set on the flesh is hostile to God, for it does not submit to God's law; indeed, it cannot" (Rom 8:7).

That God has done for you what you could never have done for yourself is the article that breaks your bondage to sin and guilt. However, that God has done for you what you could never have done for yourself is also the article that provides *ongoing* freedom and joy.

When you are weak—with a heart of repentance and humble dependence upon divine grace—you can begin to see how Jesus is your strength. He is the strongman on your behalf. He is the Adam who came to restore the effects of the Fall, the Joshua who leads you into the new Promised Land, and the David who has conquered the Goliaths of sin, death, and hell. Your weakness is the vehicle of Christ's strength. Jesus didn't come to save the righteous, but sinners.

There is a beauty found in being broken. Admit your failure, cling to the sufficiency and merits of Christ, rest in your adoption as a son or daughter of God, and your burden will be broken and you will find freedom through failure.

Discussion Questions

- What might be some of the benefits of church discipline? How might it promote a freedom through failure?

- Have you ever hit a breaking point, where you felt completely broken over your sin? What brought you comfort?

- Reflect on the definitions of "pretending" and "performing" as offered by Bob Thune and Will Walker. How might these eventually lead to bondage rather than freedom?

- What is the difference between true, biblical freedom and the freedom as oftentimes understood by the world?

- How are we to grow in holiness?

4

Risking Your Reputation

WHEN WE SEEK THE PRAISE OF OTHERS, we can easily become a *reputation chameleon*. Our reputation and identity constantly change with the surrounding environment of what makes a person popular.

As I look back at my own life, I can clearly see a pattern of changing identities as I have attempted to establish a certain reputation—soccer, rock climbing, bad boy, and scholar. My goal, so often, was not to bring glory to God, but to be known, accepted, loved, feared, and respected by a sinful and watching world.

Just when I thought I had conquered my sin of reputation, my chameleon heart quickly sought the reputation of those in the church. My reputation changed from one shade of self-righteous identity to another. I was too afraid to admit weakness and sin because I wanted to be loved and accepted by church leaders and I feared their rejection. I possessed a fear of man, not God. I experienced the old proverb: "The fear of man lays a snare, but whoever trusts in the LORD is safe" (Prov 29:25).

What would it take for you to risk your reputation?

First-Class Pharisee

Some people acquire jobs, degrees, and skills—not to impact society for good—but for the sole purpose of creating an impressive resume. To put it simply, their experience and qualifications serve themselves rather than others. The reason that I know these people even exist is because I've been one of them! Others, however, have had a similar story, even the Apostle Paul.

> In the book of Philippians, Paul lays out his resume—qualifications that established his reputation. He writes, If anyone else thinks he has reason for confidence in the flesh, I have more: circumcised on the eighth day, of the people of Israel, of the tribe of Benjamin, a Hebrew of Hebrews; as to the law, a Pharisee; as to zeal, a persecutor of the church; as to righteousness, under the law blameless. (Phil 3:4–6)

In the context of Philippians, Paul compares himself to a group of people called "Judaizers." These Judaizers sought to make themselves sort of high-class Christians by requiring those who wanted to be Christians to conform to Jewish law and custom.

Rebutting these false teachers, Paul demonstrates that he—of all people—has every right to be of a higher class and greater esteem if the criterion is one's "Jewishness." He was a Pharisee, keeper of the law of God, zealous for the purity of the Jewish faith against the "new" Christian church, and blameless in his morality.

The Pharisees had a reputation of following the law of God and the numerous additional laws they created. They wanted to be *known* as good, moral, law-abiding people—not to please God—but to garner the praise of men. And Paul was a first-class Pharisee.

Paul's "Rubbish" Reputation

Immediately after Paul lays out his impressive resume—his reputation as a blameless first-class Pharisee—he writes, "But whatever gain I had, I counted as loss for the sake of Christ" (v. 7). Let those words sink in for a moment. Whatever gain, whatever reputation required to be of first rank and esteem among the people, Paul had it! Paul's credentials matched the expected credentials of greatness and respect. And he counted all of it as *loss* for the sake of Christ.

Or, to say it another way, *he counted knowing Jesus Christ and being known by him as the greatest treasure in the universe.*

Paul adds, "Indeed, I count everything as loss because of the surpassing worth of knowing Christ Jesus my Lord" (v. 8a). He counts all of his accomplishments and qualifications as "rubbish" (v. 8b)—literally *excrement*. Paul doesn't simply risk his reputation; he considers his reputation rubbish.

Notice, too, that Paul makes a value judgment. Being known by Jesus is of infinitely greater value or worth than being known by the world. Every accomplishment and credential earned in this life, therefore, pales in comparison to our relationship with Christ by faith. We can even count it all as "loss" when compared to knowing Christ.

Reputations ebb and flow with the changing tide of self-righteous pursuits, but to be known and loved by Almighty God frees us from our chameleon heart and enables us to enjoy the only reputation that truly matters—that our name is written in the Lamb's Book of Life.

Ashamed of Jesus

We love being associated with those who receive praise. When our sports team wins a game, we wear their colors with pride. When our church is growing, we boast in its growth. When we know someone famous, we like name-dropping in social contexts. Riding the coattails of others' fame is what we do best and Jesus's disciples knew this principle all too well.

During the week leading up to his arrest and crucifixion, Jesus rides into Jerusalem on a colt to fulfill Zechariah 9:

> Rejoice greatly, O daughter of Zion! Shout aloud, O daughter of Jerusalem! Behold, your king is coming to you; righteous and having salvation is he, humble and mounted on a donkey, on a colt, the foal of a donkey. (v. 9)

The people—all thinking he will lead the Jewish people in a conquering revolt over the oppressive Romans—spread their cloaks along the road and cried out "Hosanna, Hosanna, blessed is the King who comes in the name of the Lord!" (cf. Matt 21:9).

While the scripture passages describing the triumphal entry into Jerusalem do not detail what the twelve disciples were actually doing, I can imagine that they wanted to be as close to the King as possible! Who wouldn't?

For years, Jesus had told those whom he healed not to tell anybody because his time had not yet come. Well, Jesus's time had finally come to reveal himself as the true King of kings and Lord of lords. And, yet, he came as a *humble* king—not to conquer the Romans and lead the Jews to military victory—but to conquer sin and death and to lead his sheep into the green pastures of his transformative and sovereign grace.

A little less than a week later, while his disciples were dozing off in a nearby garden, Judas Iscariot led a mob of soldiers to arrest Jesus. In a moment, his closest friends who had accompanied the conquering King's triumphal entry into Jerusalem abandoned him. Mark writes, "And they all left him and fled" (14:50).

Unfortunately, the American church today has all too often become ashamed of Jesus. We have traded his reputation for ours. We want the fame and glory. And when Jesus seems impotent and ineffective—even unpopular—in the eyes of the world, we quickly turn to gimmicks and celebrity pastors to garner reputation and the praise of man.

Left uncurbed, this trend easily changes our "Hosannas" to a collective "Crucify him!" The vain pursuit of self-righteous reputation is the necessary consequence of disbelief in a God who is mighty to save. We proudly stand with Christ when he is popular, but flee when he is not. The reason? Because we have a reputation to preserve. Are you willing to risk it for the sake of Christ?

Jesus: More Than a Risk Taker

A prostitute breaks into the room and crashes to the floor in front of Jesus, weeping. She breaks an alabaster flask of ointment open and anoints his feet, all the while wiping his feet with her tear-soaked hair.

Immediately, the Pharisees in the room began to whisper to each other, "If only Jesus knew what kind of woman this was, he wouldn't be within fifty feet of her!" In the middle of this story in Luke 7, we witness a clash of reputations.

Please don't miss the scandalous irony: Here is Jesus, the only One to whom all true esteem, honor, glory, and privilege is due—*and yet*—he humbles himself to reach out and cleanse one who was considered worthless and vile. He not only risked his reputation to save hers, he willingly and sovereignly forsook it.

Jesus regularly moved among the poor, outcast, and unclean. The Pharisees, on the other hand, would pass by on the opposite side of the road. If you think through the stories in the Gospel accounts, consider how many of Jesus's parables and associations brought out this clash of reputations, just from the gospel of Luke:

- The question over which disciple was the "greatest" (9:46–48)
- The parable of the Good Samaritan (10:25–37)
- The teaching of the narrow door (13:22–30)
- The parable of the Lost (Elder) Son (15:11–32)
- The parable of the Rich Man and Lazarus (16:19–31)
- Jesus cleansing lepers (17:11–19)
- The parable of the Pharisee and the Tax Collector (18:9–14)
- Jesus in the home of Zacchaeus (19:1–10)
- Jesus and the widow's offering (21:1–4)

And lest we forget the greatest scandal of all—when Jesus, the eternal Son of God, was nailed to a cross in between two thieves. But even this was Jesus's own doing. He laid down his life of his own accord (John 10:18).

Seven hundred years earlier, Isaiah prophesied about the Suffering Servant, the Messiah of God:

> He was despised and rejected by men; a man of sorrows, and acquainted with grief; and as one from whom men hide their faces he was despised, and we esteemed him not. . . . Because he poured out his soul to death and was numbered with the transgressors; yet he bore the sin of many. (Isa 53:3, 12)

Only Jesus could look unto the joy set before him, endure the suffering of the cross, and despise its shame (Heb 12:2). He was despised—counted worthless by the world—and numbered with the transgressors. He forsook his reputation so that you and I might be saved.

Jesus took upon himself the sinful reputation of his people, and his people are clothed in the righteous reputation that he secured. In God's sight you have the reputation of Jesus, righteous and holy. Because your reputation is secure in the hand of God Almighty, you can risk your own reputation for the benefit of others.

The Only Reputation that Truly Matters

In Luke 10, Jesus sends out seventy-two of his followers ahead of him, two by two, "into every town and place where he himself was about to go" (v. 1). Luke tells us what happened upon their return: "The seventy-two returned with joy, saying, "Lord, even the demons are subject to us in your name (v. 17)!" After Jesus acknowledged that he had indeed given them authority to do many signs and wonders, he tells them, "Nevertheless, do not rejoice in this, that the spirits are subject to you, but rejoice that your names are written in heaven" (v. 20).

Did you catch what Jesus is telling his disciples? Their joy should be grounded, not in their own power, authority, or even what they are known to do, but in God's eternal grace—that their names have been written by God in heaven!

The only reality that should awaken your heart to sing praise is the amazing grace of God in the gospel. If your joy is grounded in your accomplishments, credentials, or reputation, it is self-serving and vain. Believer, your name was written before the foundation of the world in the Lamb's

Book of Life (Rev 13:8). Risk your earthly reputation and lay hold of the only reputation that truly matters—the one secured on your behalf and received by faith alone.

The Apostle John writes in the book of Revelation, "Then I looked, and behold, on Mount Zion stood the Lamb and with him 144,000 who had his name and his Father's name written on their foreheads" (Rev 14:1). You have been marked by the name of another—one who is called Faithful and True (Rev 19:11). Since he is your reputation, "press on toward the goal for the prize of the upward call of God in Christ Jesus" (Phil 3:14).

Excurses: Preserving the Reputation of Christ

Before we leave this discussion, we need to address an obvious objection to this chapter. Throughout history, many professing Christians have brought scandal and offense to the name of Christ. Likewise, many movements have tarnished the reputation of the Christian community in the eyes of the world. The Crusades (1095–1291), the rampant immorality of the Roman Catholic Church during the Middle Ages, and the Civil Rights movement of the 1960s are some clear examples.

Thus, we need to be clear about what we are affirming and what we are denying:

- We *affirm* that our self-righteous reputation, credentials, and accomplishments should be counted as "loss" for the sake of knowing Christ.

- We *deny* risking our reputation—as Christians—in the eyes of a watching and skeptical world.

- We *affirm* that we are to lay down self-perceived rights and entitlement and lay hold of the One to whom all honor, praise, and glory are due.

- We *deny* treating the witness of the name of Christ as a trivial and low calling.

Therefore, we should be all the more careful and diligent to let our Christian witness bear testimony to our eternal salvation.

However, let's also be clear about what it means to uphold a Christian reputation. Oftentimes, Christianity is equated with morality. Admittedly, this is the fault of many Christians, but it is also presumed upon the Christian community by the watching world.

What the world needs to see in the church is not people who are simply nice, but sinners who repent and boast in the strength of Jesus on their behalf. In turn, they need to see that this covenant community of God's people will strive to risk their reputation, fame, and fortune to make Jesus famous.

Discussion Questions

- What are you known for? Why?

- Has your reputation changed over the years?

- Take a few minutes to write out or think through your resume. Would you be willing to count it all as "loss" for the sake of knowing Christ?

- Can you think of a time when you have felt ashamed of Jesus? Explain.

- Can you think of a time when you have not wanted to associate with a particular group of people because it might affect your reputation?

- Can you think of times when the church has failed to preserve the reputation of Christ to a watching world?

5

When God Doesn't Answer

(Like You Want)

I RECEIVED AN UNSOLICITED "HEALING BLANKET" in the mail a few years ago. Actually, it was a large folded-up piece of paper that *looked* like a blanket. The enclosed instructions told me to place the blanket over any part of my body that hurt and I would be healed. In fact, the testimonials provided in the packet went on to describe how frequent use of the healing blanket also brought great financial wealth!

A televangelist, who persistently told his viewers to touch the TV screen for special healing and financial freedom, once duped a friend of mine. Of course, my friend had sent in his "seed money" the previous month and so he (naturally) expected a return on his investment. "You just don't have enough faith," my friend told me when I questioned the deal. I agreed with him. But does my lack of faith make this televangelist right in his theology? Absolutely not.

Behind the flashy suits, gold furniture, and slayings in the Spirit, lies a theology that is spiritually bankrupt. At the core is a fundamental belief that places the power of man at the center of salvation history. And part of that power includes the belief that—with a strong enough faith—you can "name it, claim it." The whole world can be yours *if* you have enough faith!

The way in which one appropriates health, wealth, and prosperity is through faith-filled prayer. This belief, of course, stems from Jesus's statement: "If you ask me anything in my name, I will do it" (John 14:14; cf. 15:16; 16:23). This was the belief of the organization that sent me the healing blanket. It doesn't take into account what the Apostle John says elsewhere; that "If we ask anything according to his will he hears us" (1 John 5:14). When the end goal is self-glorification and empowerment rather than God-glorifying humility and submission, we can easily see why this whole theology is spiritually bankrupt.

What happens when you pay large sums of money into a spiritually bankrupt "ministry" only to be disillusioned, discouraged, and disoriented? Whether we realize it or not, name-it-claim-it theology (sometimes called the "health, wealth, and prosperity gospel") has made its way across the landscape of the American church—and it has affected the way we think about prayer.

Many have even given up on prayer altogether because they don't want to be let down once more. To quote Ravi Zacharias again: "The loneliest moment in life is when you just experienced the ultimate and it has let you down."

But what is really at stake? Is it simply about prayer or have we missed the gospel altogether?

Empowered for Self

Similar to the thought behind the "healing blanket," self-help books—boasting of empowerment, financial success, personal advancement, blessing, and health—have been flooding the Christian market for years. Consider some of these recent titles: *Your Best Life Now*, *It's Your Time*, *Power Thoughts*, *How to Succeed at Being Yourself*, *The Biblical Road to Blessing*, and *Release Your Destiny, Release Your Anointing*. All of these books are by well-known "celebrity," self-professing Christians.

What is amazing, in all of these books, is what you *don't* see—humility, Christ-centeredness, the centrality of justification, and boasting in weakness. The careful reader will notice that the end goal is personal blessing, not God's glory. You are empowered by God to fulfill *your* greatest earthly dreams, however lavish and self-centered they might be. And all of this can be yours for the price of a book or with a "seed" gift of $50!

Pride and Humility

We should not be surprised to find pride at the core of these books. But anytime we elevate the gifts above the Giver, it's idolatry. God has not been silent regarding his thoughts on pride and humility. Consider some of the following biblical passages:

- "For though the LORD is high, he regards the lowly, but the haughty he knows from afar" (Ps 138:6).

- "The LORD lifts up the humble; he casts the wicked to the ground" (Ps 147:6).

- "Whoever humbles himself like this child is the greatest in the kingdom of heaven" (Matt 18:4).

- "Whoever exalts himself will be humbled, and whoever humbles himself will be exalted" (Matt 23:4).

- "If anyone would be first, he must be last of all and servant of all" (Mark 10:35).

- "In humility, count others more significant than your-selves" (Phil 2:3).

- "God opposes the proud, but gives grace to the hum-ble" (Jas 4:6).

These passages show the reality and danger of a pride-ful heart. Not only does God oppose the proud, but pride is also a snare to our walk and communion with God.

If we are honest, we know that each of us holds pride in our heart. In his book, *Humility*, C. J. Mahaney writes,

> The real issue is not *if* pride exists in your heart; it's *where* pride exists and *how* pride is being expressed in your life. Scripture shows us that pride is strongly and dangerously rooted in all our lives, far more than most of us care to admit or even think about.[1]

The very fact that it is hard to admit that we are prideful is itself a banner of pride!

Whether you realize it or not, pride is always ready to raise its ugly head and express itself in the form of self-righteousness—the idea that you boast in your own righ-teousness rather than Christ's. Bob Thune and Will Walker provide some helpful insights here:[2]

- Job Righteousness: I'm a hard worker, so God will reward me.

- Family Righteousness: Because I "do things right" as a parent, I'm more godly than parents who can't control their kids.

- Intellectual Righteousness: I am better read, more articulate, and more culturally savvy than others, which obviously makes me superior.

1. Mahaney, *Humility*, 29.
2. Thune and Walker, *Gospel-Centered Life*, 14–15.

- Schedule Righteousness: I am self-disciplined and rigorous in my time management, which makes me more mature than others.

- Flexibility Righteousness: In a world that's busy, I'm flexible and relaxed. I always make time for others. Shame on those who don't!

- Mercy Righteousness: I care about the poor and disadvantaged the way everyone else should.

- Financial Righteousness: I manage money wisely and stay out of debt. I'm not like those materialistic Christians who can't control their spending.

- Political Righteousness: I know my candidate is the best and if you really loved God you'd vote for him too.

- Tolerance Righteousness: I am open-minded and charitable toward those who don't agree with me. In fact, I'm a lot like Jesus that way!

If you're like me, several of these hit home. All of these self-righteous tendencies are the outward workings of pride and its cousin, unbelief. Together, they form the twin roots of all actual sins.

Think about these two "root" sins for a moment. You cannot exalt Christ if you are exalting yourself. Similarly, when a person is plagued by unbelief, he or she ends up trusting in his or her own strength—which is pride.

Humility, on the other hand, is a forgetting of yourself in the grace and truth of God. It's a deep-seated desire and delight in God, which translates into selfless expression. It's the idea captured in Philippians 3:8, where Paul writes, "I count everything as loss because of the surpassing worth of knowing Christ Jesus my lord." It's the feeling David expresses in Psalm 63:1–3:

> O God, you are my God; earnestly I seek you;
> my soul thirsts for you; my flesh faints for you,
> as in a dry and weary land where there is no
> water. So I have looked upon you in the sanctu-
> ary, beholding your power and glory. Because
> your steadfast love is better than life, my lips will
> praise you.

Did you catch that? A singular focus upon the glory and majesty of God and a delight in his manifold perfections eclipses our own pursuit of self-glory. The bright noonday sun of the glory of God simply overwhelms the light cast by our flickering candles.

Prayer is a battlefield between pride and humility. It is where we lay down our self-righteousness and acknowledge our complete and utter dependence upon divine grace. We should reflect the humility of the tax collector who cried out, "God, be merciful to me, a sinner!" and not the self-sufficiency of the Pharisee (Luke 18:9–14).

When we pray to the living, true, and sovereign God of the universe, pride *must* flee. And when God doesn't answer *like we want*, we come humbly again before his throne of grace—laying our selfish desires down before his perfectly wise and powerful plan.

Praying According to the Will of God

We are called to pray according to God's will. The Apostle John writes, "If we ask anything according to his will he hears us" (1 John 5:14). This, then, begs the question: How can we *know* the will of God? First, let's define "will."

The idea of "will" is used in several distinct ways in Christian theology. First, there is the immutable, eternal, and decretal will of God that stands as his absolute plan brought forth by his sovereign power and providence.

Second, there is the will of God that reveals his commandments or those things he takes delight in. For example, it
is God's will that you worship him and not steal or com-
mit adultery. Third, there is simple volition, which may be
defined as desire of sufficient intensity that's translated into
action.[3]

Here, in 1 John, the second idea is employed—that
which God has commanded or what he takes delight in.
Our prayers should dovetail and be informed by the expressed command and delight of God. Where do we find
God's revelation of his commands and delights? The word
of God. Our prayers, therefore, should attest to the truth of
scripture.

When we pray, then, we should come humbly, yet
boldly, before the throne of grace (Heb 4:16), bringing
our petitions (Phil 4:6) as his adopted children (Gal 4:6)—
trusting in the manifold wisdom of God (Eph 3:10), in his
eternal purposes (Isa 46:10), and in his steadfast love for his
people (Ps 100:5).

If our prayers are marked by the above attributes—
which is "according to God's will"—then we should not
be disillusioned or disheartened by the desired "outcome."
While we are called to bring our requests and petitions to
God in faith, we should affirm Christ's own affirmation of
his Father's will before his arrest and subsequent crucifixion: "Nevertheless, not my will, but yours, be done" (Luke
22:42).

Prayers of adoration, confession, thanksgiving, sup-
plication, and intercession should all bow before a sovereign God who has united us to himself through the work of
his son, Jesus Christ. In this way, our prayers affirm God's
will over us and for us.

3. This third idea of "will" is helpfully described in Peck, *Road
Less Traveled*, 83.

Prayer as a "Means of Grace"

Prayer is also a means by which God grows our faith, mortifies our sin, and brings us into greater communion with him. In this sense, prayer has historically been called a "means of grace."[4] But prayer doesn't bring us into greater communion with God *ex opera operato*—just by doing it. In other words, just because you pray doesn't necessarily mean that you will grow in faith. But God delights to use prayer as a means to grow us in our faith.

D. G. Hart and John Muether write, "When we offer up our requests to God for things agreeable to his will, then our prayers will be a blessing to us and cause us to grow in grace."[5] Praying according to God's will not only brings our desires and delights into conformity with God's desires and delights; God uses such prayer to grow his children in grace.

Pleading with the Lord—In Weakness

In the book of Isaiah—which weaves prophecy of judgment together with deliverance of God's people—the prophet describes Israel's faith when they find themselves in distress. He writes, "O LORD, in distress they sought you; *they poured out a whispered prayer* when your discipline was upon them" (Isa 26:16, italics mine). Have you ever poured out a "whispered prayer" in times of distress? This is a prayer that comes from desperation and an acknowledgment of dependence.

We find a similar idea in the New Testament. In the previous chapters of this book, we have been exploring Paul's "thorn in the flesh" from 2 Corinthians 12. In verse

4. Cf. The *Westminster Larger Catechism*, Question 154.
5. Hart and Muether, *With Reverence and Awe*, 142.

8, Paul writes of his desire for this thorn to be removed: "Three times I pleaded with the Lord about this, that it should leave me."

The word Paul uses for "pleaded" (*parakaleo*) is a Greek word filled with emotion and urgency. This is not a mere request; it is a plea for mercy. It is the casting of oneself down in complete dependence upon Another. Paul, here, comes to the Lord in weakness, but full of faith, trusting in the strength of Christ.

Do you ever resonate with Paul's *pleading*? Have you ever been at the end of yourself, to the point of throwing up your hands and asking for the mercy of God in your life? Have you ever been so burdened during the night that you come to the point of complete and utter acknowledgement of your own inadequacy and need for divine grace?

There is something beautiful and pure about this kind of heartfelt, urgent, pleading prayer. In the middle of your greatest weakness, you come to the One who is supremely strong. All of the sudden, when everything around you seems to be crumbling, you come upon the Solid Rock, as seen in the lines of the hymn by the same name:

> His oath, His covenant, His blood
> Support me in the whelming flood.
> When all around my soul gives way,
> He then is all my Hope and Stay
> And it is precisely *in* those times when everything around you gives way *that* you see Jesus *as* your hope and stay. When you are weak, boasting in the surety of your salvation—Jesus Christ—makes you strong.

Discussion Questions

- How might "health, wealth, and prosperity" teaching promote a self-centered, self-glorifying prayer life?

- What is the attitude with which we are to approach God in prayer?

- What does it mean to pray "according to the will of God"?

- How is prayer a "means of grace"?

- Can you think of a time when you have *pleaded* with the Lord about a particular struggle in your life?

6

My Grace Is Sufficient for You

GRACE IS VERY ANTI EVOLUTIONARY. In fact, the existence of grace is probably one of the strongest arguments against evolutionary theory. Survival of the fittest—the stronger eating the weak—doesn't float in the sea of grace. The reason is not because grace is too regressive to the "higher forms" of life, but because grace assumes the payment of another—something completely counter intuitive, counter evolutionary. Let me explain.

When I was younger, my family would visit my aunt and uncle each summer in South Georgia. On one particular visit, I found a new (and expensive!) porcelain vase sitting on an end table, which my aunt had purchased for the guest bedroom. As I examined the colorful pattern, the vase suddenly slipped out of my hands and crashed to the floor—sending out an explosion of tiny pieces all over the room. I felt horrible and I knew that I would have to use all of my money from mowing yards that summer to purchase a replacement vase.

But, to my surprise, my aunt insisted that she would take care of it; *she would cover the cost to replace it*. She wouldn't even let my parents pay for it! She was gracious toward me and her grace was expressed by taking the cost of a new vase upon herself.

God has expressed this kind of grace in the gospel of Jesus Christ. He redeems us and brings us into his family—even when we had shattered our relationship with him through sin—at infinite cost to himself. As a pastor once said, God sent his only son, Jesus Christ, to pay a debt that he did not owe, for us, who had a debt that we could never pay. This kind of action goes against the message and propaganda of this fallen world. And it's the kind of action that magnifies the strength of Christ in the weakness of man.

When I turned seven years old, my father bought me a BB gun. I grew up shooting guns so I was comfortable with the idea, but this was my very own gun. You could have heard the squirrels and rabbits within a mile of my home scurry for cover!

When visiting my grandfather's home one day, I was immediately presented with a large target: a four-by-six-foot window on the side of a water-pump building. (Looking back, I'm sure I left my thinking cap under a rock somewhere.) That large window—reflecting the bright sunlight—didn't have a chance against my BB gun. With one quick shot, that window was history. But then it suddenly dawned on me; I was going to have to confess what I did to my grandfather!

I slowly walked down to my grandfather's house, through the front door, and into the kitchen where he was reading. "Granddaddy," I said sheepishly.

"Yes," he said, looking up from his book.

I didn't know where to start, so it just fumbled out: "I shot the water-pump window and it broke and I'm very sorry." I immediately began to cry out of shame and guilt.

He put down his book, got up from his chair, and knelt down beside me. "Thank you for telling me, Brian. Don't worry about the window. I'll take care of it. I appreciate your honesty."

My grandfather taught me something about grace that day. I deserved punishment. I deserved to make the payment for the window. But he whom I had offended became the very one who covered the cost for my offense.

In the same way, the One whom I have offended by my sin became the very One who paid the price for my sin. As Paul writes in Romans 5:8, "God shows his love for us in that while we were still sinners, Christ died for us." God didn't wait for me to get it all together. He didn't wait for me to rack up enough good-works points or clean up my act. No, he came in and saved me while I was in open rebellion to him. That's grace. That's God's unmerited favor.

The Answer

In the last chapter, we examined prayer and how God sometimes doesn't answer our prayers like we want him to. In this chapter, we will briefly examine Jesus's answer to Paul's *pleading* in 2 Corinthians 12:8. If you remember, the Apostle Paul pleads with the Lord three times to have this "thorn" in the flesh removed. This "pleading" is not a casual, heartless prayer, but a visceral, emotive, and deep plea for divine mercy—he wants his burden lifted.

But Jesus gives Paul an answer that is completely shocking. He tells Paul, "My grace is sufficient for you, for my power is made perfect in weakness" (v. 9).

Reread that verse again slowly.

Notice what Jesus *doesn't* tell Paul. He doesn't say, "Sure, Paul, I'll remove that thorn for you." The answer Paul received from Jesus probably wasn't what he wanted to hear. He asked for his thorn to be removed, but Jesus didn't answer like he wanted.

Nor did Jesus say, "No, Paul, deal with it. You call that a *thorn*!" Jesus's answer is neither superficial nor harsh. It powerfully penetrates the darkness of Paul's problem, pain, and weakness. But what *does* Jesus say to Paul? Let's take a look at Jesus's two-part answer.

My Grace is Sufficient—*For You!*

The first part of Jesus's answer is simply, "My grace is sufficient for you" (2 Cor 12:9). Have you ever wondered why Jesus brings up the topic of *grace* during a time of turmoil and struggle? Grace is getting what we don't deserve; unmerited favor. Why does Jesus speak of grace when Paul seems to be struggling with a heavy burden or "thorn"? Can it be that part of Paul's struggle is a struggle with sin? I think so. While we are not exactly sure what this "thorn" is (as we have already discussed), the fact that the thorn is given to keep him from further sin could easily be either a physical ailment or a personal struggle with sin. In fact, the two often come together!

The Apostle Paul regularly speaks of his sin. Other than his pre-conversion days, he doesn't describe his sin in any detail. He simply speaks in general terms: "Christ Jesus came into the world to save sinners, of whom I am the foremost" (1 Tim 1:15); "I have the desire to do what is right, but not he ability to carry it out . . . when I want to do right, evil lies close at hand" (Rom 7:18, 22).

In the context of 2 Corinthians 12, we've seen how Paul struggled with spiritual pride. It was precisely because of his temptation with spiritual pride that he was given a "thorn in his flesh"—to keep him humble! The reason that Christ speaks of grace is because the thorn is actually an expression of divine grace to keep him humble *and* it is to Christ that Paul is to turn in the midst of his struggle and pain. That he even had One to turn to is also an expression of divine grace!

55

The truth revealed in this passage is similar to that which we find in the hymn, "How Firm a Foundation." Consider the words to a few of the verses:

> Fear not I'm with thee O be not dismayed
> For I am thy God I will still give thee aid
> I'll strengthen thee help thee,
>   and cause thee to stand
> Upheld by My gracious omnipotent hand
>
> When through the deep waters
>   He calls thee to go
> The rivers of grief shall not thee overflow
> For He will be with thee in trouble to bless
> And sanctify to thee thy deepest distress
>
> When through fiery trials thy pathway shall lie
> My grace all-sufficient shall be thy supply
> The flames shall not hurt thee I only design
> Thy dross to consume and thy gold to refine

Did you catch the key idea? "When through fiery trials thy pathway shall lie; My grace all-sufficient shall be thy supply." John Calvin writes in his commentary on 2 Corinthians 12:9, "The valleys are watered with rain to make them fruitful, while in the meantime; the high summits of the lofty mountains remain dry. Let that man, therefore, become a valley, who is desirous to receive the heavenly rain of God's spiritual grace."[1]

This is the message that Jesus communicates to Paul. In the midst of Paul's sin, pain, and burden, the grace of Christ becomes his only supply. He cannot trust in his own merits, accomplishments, talents, or accolades. Jesus breaks through all of our self-righteousness with the message, "You are upheld by my gracious omnipotent hand."

---

1. Calvin, *Calvin's Bible Commentaries*, 288.

Notice one more element about Jesus's response to Paul. He says, "My grace is sufficient *for you* (italics mine)." Jesus's grace is intentional, purposeful, and personal. It is not an arbitrary or platonic pie-in-the-sky abstract idea. No, the grace of Christ is sufficient *for you*; yes, even for you! There is no condemnation for those who are in Christ Jesus (Rom 8:1). Believer,

> Do you struggle with pride?
>   There is no condemnation for you.
> Do you struggle with pornography?
>   There is no condemnation for you.
> Do you struggle with alcohol or drugs?
>   There is no condemnation for you.
> Do you struggle with anger?
>   There is no condemnation for you.
> Do you struggle with envy?
>   There is no condemnation for you.

> When the thorns of sin and shame seem to choke out your joy, Jesus comes and speaks a word of pardon over you—"My grace, all sufficient, shall be thy supply."

It's interesting to note, too, that Jesus's response to Paul is in the present or progressive tense—"My grace is sufficient for you." He doesn't say that his grace *was* sufficient or *will be* sufficient. In the present, in the now, in the moment of sin and despair, the grace of Christ *is* sufficient. Grace doesn't dry up and run out. It is an ever-flowing stream of life for those who come and drink.

The Power of Christ

The second part of Jesus's answer has caused some confusion, "For my power is made perfect in weakness" (2 Cor

12:9). How is Christ's power made perfect . . . in weakness? What is the "power" that he speaks of?

The word Paul uses in Greek for power is *dynamis*—where we get the English word "dynamite." The grace of Christ comes and explodes the thorns of sin and shame. But how does this happen theologically? It happens in two ways, one immediately and one gradually.

In the immediate sense, the grace of God causes us to be born again (1 Pet 1:3) and declares us "righteous" in his sight. How? God made him—Jesus—who knew no sin to *be* sin for us, so that in him we might become the righteousness of God (2 Cor 5:21). Therefore, Paul can speak of our justification in the *past* tense—"Since we have been justified by faith, we have peace with God through our Lord Jesus Christ" (Rom 5:1). The power of Christ is seen first by conquering the "lesser" powers of sin, death, and hell forever—for his bride, his sheep. Christ's accomplishment and work, credited to the people of God and received by faith alone, is the immediate and initial "power" that Paul experiences in his salvation.

However, there is also an *ongoing* power of Christ—one that gradually or progressively mortifies our sin and conforms us more and more into his image. This progressive and gradual process is called sanctification. It is the work of God's free grace in making us into that which we have already been declared—holy and righteous in his sight. The holiness of God becomes the ground on which he demands holiness in us (cf. 1 Pet 1:16) and he demands nothing less than perfection (Matt 5:48).

Therefore, the power of Christ is not only displayed in the *salvation* of his bride, but also in the *cleansing* of his bride: "Christ loved the church and gave himself up for her, that he might sanctify her" (Eph 5:25). But how is this "power" made perfect in weakness?

Power Made Perfect in Weakness

In 2 Corinthians 12:9, Jesus tells Paul that his grace is sufficient for him and that his power is "made perfect in weakness." As a magnifying glass brings into sight that which it magnifies, so our weaknesses magnify Christ's power on our behalf.

When we consider the weakness/power contrast in biblical theology—especially the New Testament—we find something remarkable when we consider our union with Christ in his death and resurrection. The eternal Son of God entered into our weakness in his incarnation. He became flesh (John 1:14), humbled himself to the point of death, even death on a cross (Phil 2:8). As Paul writes, "He was crucified in weakness, but lives by the power of God" (2 Cor 13:4). What is the result and effect for all who place their faith and trust in him? It is eternal salvation and the resurrection of the body to new life in Christ: "It is sown in weakness; it is raised in power" (1 Cor 15:43).

Jesus tells Paul, "My power is made perfect in weakness." Here is the meaning. Please don't miss this profound truth: *Paul's weakness is the stage for Christ's strength.* It is precisely in weakness that the strength and power of Christ is most gloriously displayed. Paul, then, becomes an arrow—pointing to him who is King *and* Servant, Lion *and* Lamb.

A remarkable phenomenon in our culture takes place, when confronted with weakness: we want to escape. John Piper, in a sermon on this text, explains: "One of the reasons biblical Christianity has to be so drastically distorted in order to sell it to mass markets is that the market wants power to escape weakness in leisure." He adds, "What the market wants is escape from weakness, not power in weakness."[2]

2. Piper, "Christ's Power is Made Perfect."

Let us look to Jesus, then, the author and perfecter of our faith, who doesn't *escape* the weakness and suffering of the cross, but rather drinks the full cup of God's wrath for us (cf. Heb 12:2). He is forsaken so that we will enjoy communion and fellowship with the living God.

So to summarize: *Jesus's weakness on the cross becomes the source of our strength. Our weakness in sin is the platform for his strength in us.* Boasting in the strength of Jesus, therefore, is grace provided when you are weak: "My grace is sufficient for you, for my power is made perfect in weakness."

Discussion Questions

- Have you ever pleaded with the Lord about a particular burden and not getting the "answer" you expected?

- Can you think of a time when you have been shown grace? What about a time that you have shown grace to another?

- Reread the stanzas from the hymn, "How Firm a Foundation." What lines do you see as particularly striking and poignant?

- Other than blaspheming the Holy Spirit (rejecting the effectual work of the Spirit's work in salvation), do you feel that some sins are simply beyond the grace of God?

- What is meant by the "power" of Christ?

- How is weakness a stage or a platform for Christ's strength?

7

Forsaking Your Fear of Weakness

OVER THE LAST TWENTY YEARS or so we have seen a re-
discovery of the rich literature of the seventeenth-century
English Puritans. Books by John Bunyan, John Owen, Richard Baxter, John Flavel, and Richard Sibbes now grace the
shelves in many homes of pastors, teachers, and laypeople.

One of the most helpful resources to be published is a
collection of Puritan prayers, entitled *The Valley of Vision*,
edited by Arthur Bennett. In the opening prayer, "The Valley of Vision," we get a glimpse of the paradoxical nature of
weakness and strength, of difficulty and delight, of lows and
highs. I quote it here at length:

> Lord, high and holy, meek and lowly, Thou hast
> brought me to the valley of vision, where I live in
> the depths but see Thee in the heights; hemmed
> in by mountains of sin I behold Thy glory. Let me
> learn by paradox that the way down is the way
> up, that to be low is to be high, that the broken
> heart is the healed heart, that the contrite spirit
> is the rejoicing spirit, that the repenting soul is
> the victorious soul, that to have nothing is to
> possess all, that to bear the cross is to wear the
> crown, that to give is to receive, that the valley
> is the place of vision. Lord, in the daytime stars
> can be seen from deepest wells, and the deeper

the wells the brighter Thy stars shine; let me find
Thy light in my darkness, Thy life in my death,
Thy joy in my sorrow, Thy grace in my sin, Thy
riches in my poverty, Thy glory in my valley.[1]

In 2 Corinthians 12, the Apostle Paul is brought to
the *valley of vision*. It's in his low estate and humble circumstances that Jesus speaks a word of grace into his life.
Wanting to escape the burden of his "thorn in the flesh,"
Paul pleads three times for the Lord to remove it. But, as
we examined in the last chapter, Jesus's response of power
and grace met Paul exactly where he was—in his weakness.

In this chapter, we will examine Paul's response to
Christ's grace in 2 Corinthians 12:9: "Therefore I will boast
all the more gladly of my weaknesses, so that the power of
Christ may rest upon me." We will see that this response—
inspired by the Holy Spirit—sets a biblical pattern for living
and leading others in the twenty-first century.

The Folly of Fear

We fear all kinds of things—spiders, snakes, burglars, punishment, taxes, police, public speaking, heights, and the
like. The Bible speaks of these kinds of fears, but a biblical
theology of fear necessarily includes a deeper understanding of fear as well—especially the fear of God and the fear
of man.

From the outset, we need to understand that there is
a wrong fear and a right fear. Wrong (sinful) fear, according to scripture, is an emotion whose foundation is *faithless
idolatry*. Let me explain.

This kind of fear lacks faith; he or she does not believe that God is really in control and that all things work

1. Bennett, *Valley of Vision*, x.

for good for those who love him and are called according to his purpose (Rom 8:28). This sinful fear, put simply, is idolatry. It's idolizing your own safety, wealth, and health. It's exchanging the glory of God for your own reputation, status, and security. Any threat to these things brings fear because they have been elevated to a sinful place in your worship and affection.

Scripture tells us, "The fear of man lays a snare, but whoever trusts in the LORD is safe" (Prov 29:25). How does the fear of man lay a snare? Jamie Munson, in his article, "8 Snares Set by Fear of Man," gives some insight. When we fear man, Munson argues, it can lead to the following eight "snares," which I'll summarize here:[2]

1. Idolatry—We seek to please others and win their approval instead of seeking to please God and rest in his approval.

2. Ineffectiveness—Because we become too preoccupied with what others think of us, we lose sight of the tasks at hand.

3. Lack of love—When we fear man, we turn people into projects and our compassion fades.

4. Fakeness—If we're always trying to be accepted by others, we will be a chameleon, changing masks to fit the expectations of others.

5. Apathy—Out of fear of failure before others, we will cease to take risks and settle into a life with little to no significant action.

6. Dishonesty—It's difficult to tell others the truth, especially if that truth is painful and we fear what they might think, say, or do.

2. Munson, "8 Snares Set by Fear."

7. Isolation—Delegating responsibility may lead to someone doing either a bad job or a better job, both hurting
our reputation.

8. Decision paralysis—When we live out of fear of others
rather than a sense of divine calling, it is very difficult
to move forward.

The passage in Proverbs contrasts the fear of man with
trusting God. In other words, if we are fearing man, then
we are not trusting God. But if we are trusting God, we do
not fear man. They are antithetical realities.

The fear of the Lord, on the other hand, is highly
praised throughout scripture. David writes, "Oh, fear the
LORD, you his saints, for those who fear him have no lack"
(Ps 34:9). "The steadfast love of the LORD is from everlasting to everlasting on those who fear him" (Ps 103:17). "The
fear of the LORD is the beginning of wisdom" (Ps 111:10;
cf. Prov 1:7; 9:10). What does fearing the Lord mean?

Fearing the Lord is faithfully living in the knowledge
of the holy with awe and wonder. Such an approach is the
beginning of wisdom because it views life from a heavenly
perspective. It sets the priorities straight because it keeps
the glory of God as its chief aim. The fear of God produces
wisdom, wisdom produces joy, and joy in God brings him
glory. And so we accomplish that *chief end* for which we
were created—to glorify God and enjoy him forever!

But there is also a direct relationship between the love
of God and the fear of man. The Apostle John writes, "There
is no fear in love, but perfect love casts out fear" (1 John
4:18). If you know and hold to the promise that you are
loved and accepted unconditionally by God, such love dis-
pels the feeling of fear. God's perfect love is like light burst-
ing into a dark room, immediately dispelling the darkness.
Fear can't hold a candle to the light of God's perfect love.

Why bring this discussion of fear into a chapter about boasting in weakness? The reason that I bring up this issue about fear is because *we often struggle to boast in weakness precisely because we fear others.* One of the primary reasons that we fail to do what Paul pledges to do in 2 Corinthians 12:9 is because we are afraid of losing our reputation and looking foolish in the eyes of the world.

Paul understands that his gospel message *will* be foolish in the eyes of the world: "For the word of the cross is folly to those who are perishing, but to us who are being saved it is the power of God" (1 Cor 1:18). Paul adds that God has chosen to save his people "through the folly of what we preach" (v. 21). He knows that we, as believers, are counted "fools for Christ's sake" (1 Cor 4:10).

The burdensome quest to *attain* and *maintain* a certain reputation—apart from Christ—sets ablaze the kindling of the fear of man. As the martyred missionary Jim Elliot once wrote, "He is no fool who gives what he cannot keep to gain that which he cannot lose."[3] The irony here should not be missed. Allow me to tweak Elliot's quote a bit, showing the reverse and the effects of pursuing the vanity of reputation out of fear of others:

> He *is* a fool who neglects what he cannot earn
> (God's acceptance) to gain what he cannot keep
> (the world's acceptance).

When we realize that God's perfect, unconditional, and never-letting-go love is our greatest reputation, joy, and crown, then his love casts out fear and opens the door to gladly boasting in weakness.

---

3. Quoted in Elisabeth Elliot, *Shadow of the Almighty*, 108.

Gladly Boasting in Weakness(es)

Paul writes, in response to the sufficiency of Jesus's grace, "I will boast all the more gladly of my weaknesses" (2 Cor 12:9). Boasting in weakness is one thing; boasting *gladly* in weakness is another thing. Paul's statement captures both the intent and the action of his boasting.

But notice, too, that he says "weaknesses," plural. Paul doesn't simply let generic weakness suffice for his boasting. He intends to get specific. There are individual weaknesses and he's going to gladly boast about them. It doesn't cost you much to boast generally about sin—"I'm a sinner." It costs you much more to confess a specific sin.

Would *you* gladly boast of your anger management problems, how much time you spend in front of the TV, how much you lust, how you don't treat your spouse like you know he or she should be treated? These are specific and it takes a certain amount of vulnerability and confidence in knowing *whose* you are to boast in weakness*es*.

Do you have somebody that you can get specific with—somebody that knows you and loves you anyway?

Gladly boasting is much more than merely "telling" somebody about weaknesses. We can't forget that it's a *glad boasting* about weaknesses. Why would Paul employ these words? Why couldn't he just say, "I'm going to tell others about my weaknesses"? The reason why I think he specifically mentions a glad boasting is because there is great freedom and joy in *expressing* trust in Christ. I can say, "I trust Christ" all day long, but when I put that trust to action—when it is *expressed*—then I experience great freedom and joy. Let me illustrate.

When I was in college, I joined a fraternity. My initial intention was to be a witness for Christ to this fraternity. However, after a year, I realized that I was being pulled down more than I was pulling others up. I truly sought the Lord in prayer and sought wisdom from some close Christian friends. More than that, I trusted in my identity and security as an adopted child of God. I knew I needed to get out of the fraternity and the date was set.

On that particular evening, I stood before the entire chapter and told them that I was leaving the fraternity and why. I confessed my sin and weakness before them and I got specific. Immediately, the fraternity brothers became enraged and began yelling at me and told me to leave. For several weeks after, I would find my tires removed from my car, I was repeatedly cussed out during my classes, and generally ostracized by those who had been my "friends" only days before.

However, as I left the fraternity house the evening I told them I was leaving, I had tremendous peace, freedom, and joy. I was honest about my weakness and felt the presence and delight of God. I clung to the fact that I was his child. Yes, I knew I was weak. But I also knew Christ was strong on my behalf.

In those trying days and weeks, I was living Psalm 55:22: "Cast your burden on the LORD, and he will sustain you." I was realizing the truth of Psalm 68:19: "Blessed be the LORD, who daily bears us up." I was praying Psalm 71:3: "Be a rock of refuge, to which I may continually come." And through it all, I experienced God's smile and delight.

In the movie *Chariots of Fire*, there is a scene where the main character, Eric Liddell, is having a discussion with his sister, Jenny, about whether or not he should continue on his Olympic running career or quit and become a missionary to China. He tells his sister, "Jenny, Jenny. God's made me for a purpose, for China. But he's also made me fast; and when I run, I feel his pleasure."

Boasting in weakness becomes *glad* boasting in weakness when you see the end for which you are boasting—fellowship and communion with the greatest treasure in the universe, Jesus Christ. "For his sake," Paul writes in Philippians, "I have suffered the loss of all things and count them as rubbish, in order that I may gain Christ and be found in him" (Phil 3:8–9). May you experience the freedom and joy of boasting in weakness so that the power of Christ may rest sweetly upon you.

Covered by the Gracious Power of Christ

Before we leave this discussion of Paul's response to Christ's grace, we need to take note of Paul's last statement: "So that the power of Christ may rest upon me" (2 Cor 12:9). Paul sought to gladly boast of his weaknesses *so that* the power of Christ might rest upon him. There was a purpose for which Paul gladly boasted—the communing presence of the power of Christ. What does that mean?

Let's take a quick step back. In boasting "gladly" of weakness, Paul is not saying that such boasting necessarily *feels* good. Rather, such boasting carries with it Christ's assurance that it will *produce* good in our communion with him. There is, therefore, something sweet and joyous about boasting in weaknesses because it leads to greater communion and fellowship with the One who is strong on our behalf. Christ's gracious power is effectual in our expressed trust in him; namely, in boasting of our weaknesses.

In Matthew 13:44, Jesus tells the parable of the Hidden Treasure to describe the surpassing worth of knowing him. Jesus says, "The kingdom of heaven is like the treasure hidden in a field, which a man found and covered up. Then *in his joy* he goes and sells all that he has and buys that field" (italics mine).

Selling all that he had probably didn't bring the man joy, in and of itself. But selling all that he had in order to gain something so much greater brought him great joy, even in the selling of his possessions!

Similarly, like the man who joyfully sells all he has to buy the field with the treasure, so Paul joyfully boasts in his weaknesses to "buy" (without money) the experience of resting in the grace and power of Christ (cf. Isa 55:1). The actual boasting in weaknesses doesn't bring joy in and of itself; *it's the treasure for which we boast in weakness that brings joy into the boasting.*

Paul sought to boast because he wanted to rest in the powerful grace of Christ. Jesus had become his Righteousness. Jesus had become his very life, which is why Paul could say, "For to me, to live is Christ" (Phil 1:21). When we are weak, boasting in Jesus—his merit, his grace, and his power—makes us strong.

Discussion Questions

- Do you find anything particularly striking about the opening prayer, "The Valley of Vision"?

- What is the difference between sinful fear and godly fear?

- How does the fear of man prohibit us from boasting in weakness?

- How does God's perfect, never-letting-go love cast out fear?

- How does boasting in weakness translate to *gladly* boasting in weakness?

8

Being Content in God

"WHAT DOES GOD WANT WITH MY MONEY, ANYWAY?" I thought, watching the offering plate pass over me. My third-grade mind knew that if God had created the world, he could certainly create some cash for his divine wallet. But the preacher told us, "Give back to God his tithes." *His* tithe? It was *my* money—my grandparents gave it to me for Christmas! What I didn't realize at the time was what Jesus said in his Sermon on the Mount, "Where your treasure is, there your heart will be also" (Matt 6:21). I did not treasure God at the time and, therefore, I did not find contentment and satisfaction in him.

In the previous chapters, we have been unpacking 2 Corinthians 12, particularly verses 7–9. These verses illustrate Paul's burden by a "thorn in the flesh," which he calls a "messenger of Satan." But he is firm that this burden, this thorn, is a gracious providence of God to keep him humble and dependent. We've also examined Paul's desperate pleading with the Lord to remove it, Jesus's gracious response, and Paul's desire to boast in his weaknesses.

In this chapter, we will examine the last verse in this passage, verse 10: "For the sake of Christ, then, I am content with weaknesses, insults, hardships, persecutions, and calamities. For when I am weak, then I am strong." As we will see, the key to understanding our strength in God is in understanding our contentment in God.

Contentment with Godliness

Contentment is a feeling and state that does not come easily. Throughout the Old Testament, we see a long line of discontent. A third of the angels of heaven did not learn contentment and so fell with Satan. Adam and Eve in the garden did not learn contentment and so ate of the forbidden fruit. The people of Israel, wandering in the desert, did not learn contentment and so despaired of life even when God had provided manna and quail. King David did not learn contentment, seeking the wife of another, and so spiraled down into greater and greater sin. Solomon, with all of his wealth and women, did not learn contentment, and so followed the idols and gods of the land.

Despite these examples of *dis*contentment, we see the promises of God in supplying our every need. Indeed, there is an art of *learning* divine contentment. The Apostle Paul writes to the Philippians—while in chains—"I have learned in whatever situation I am to be content" (Phil 4:11). By grace, Paul *learned* the art of contentment. His life was wrapped up in Christ. Earlier in his letter to the Philippians, he writes, "But whatever gain I had, I counted as loss for the sake of Christ. Indeed, I count everything as loss because of the surpassing worth of knowing Christ Jesus my Lord" (Phil 3:7–8). Paul suffered the loss of earthly possessions and, yet, could say that he is content. How so?

First off, we need to realize that contentment, by itself, is not enough. Paul tells Timothy, "Now there is great gain in godliness with contentment" (1 Tim 6:6). A life of contentment confirms and seals our spoken confession of faith. Contentment is an expression of "godliness" and there is great *gain*, Paul argues, in being content in God. In other words, *our growth as Christians should be marked by a growing contentment in God*. Or, to put it negatively, a dying unto discontentment should be a mark of our dying unto sin. And the relationship to God's grace and our growth in contentment is that God's grace not only *saves* us; it *trains* us to pursue holiness (Titus 2:11–12). Contentment, then, is a holy fruit that grows in the garden of divine grace.

When we pursue holiness or righteousness, we are satisfied because God is the wellspring of all that is good and righteous. As Jesus taught his disciples, "Blessed are those who hunger and thirst for righteousness, for they shall be satisfied" (Matt 5:6). We are blessed with a satisfied and contented soul when we pursue the One who is called Righteous and Holy.

In his book, *The Art of Divine Contentment*, the Puritan Thomas Watson explains that any true contentment must be contentment *in God*. He writes, "To live contended upon God in the deficiency of comforts is an art which 'flesh and blood hath not revealed.'"[1] He adds:

> That ship that lies at anchor may sometimes be a little shaken, but never sinks. Flesh and blood may have its fears and disquiets, but grace checks them. Having cast anchor in heaven, a Christian's heart never sinks. A gracious spirit is a contended spirit.[2]

It needs to be noted, however, that we should be sensible to our circumstances. We are not stoics. When suffering comes upon us, we are called to cast ourselves upon the mercy of God. The psalmists often complained *to* God about their circumstances, though they never complained

1. Watson, *Art of Divine Contentment*, 16.
2. Ibid., 15.

about God to others. Jesus himself, when struck by the gravity of his forthcoming suffering, sweats drops of blood. He is fully aware of his circumstances. Even still, he submits his will to his Father in heaven.

Contentment, then, is an expression of godliness. They go together. It is a right response to circumstances because it shows forth the true treasure of the soul. It tangibly displays and expresses the first and greatest commandment—to love the Lord your God with all of your heart, soul, mind, and strength (Luke 10:27). In fact, *dis*contentment is gaining the whole world, but losing your soul (Matt 16:26). Let us *learn*, therefore, how to be content in God by being satisfied in God.

Satisfied in God

Scripture is replete with references to finding satisfaction and delight in God, especially the Psalms. Consider the harmony of the psalmists:

- "In your presence there is fullness of joy; at your right hand are pleasures forevermore" (16:11).

- "The LORD is my shepherd; I shall not want" (23:1).

- "Delight yourself in the LORD, and he will give you the desires of your heart" (37:4).

- "O God, you are my God, earnestly I seek you; my soul thirsts for you; my flesh faints for you, as in a dry and weary land where there is no water" (63:1).

- "Blessed is the one you choose and bring near, to dwell in your courts! We shall be satisfied with the goodness of your house, the holiness of your temple!" (65:4).

- "Satisfy us in the morning with your steadfast love" (90:14).

- "Bless the LORD . . . who satisfies you with good" (103:2, 5).

- "For he satisfies the longing soul, and the hungry soul he fills with good things" (107:9).

What is interesting in all of these verses is that delight, joy, and satisfaction are to be found in God. But even when God provides for our needs—physical and spiritual—we are to recognize that God is our great provider.

I remember several years ago going on a mission trip in Cherokee, North Carolina. After three long days of teaching and serving the Cherokee, I was weary, tired, and overwhelmed. On the fourth day, I woke up and, peradventure, came upon Psalm 90:14: "Satisfy us in the morning with your steadfast love." At reading this, I paused and echoed that prayer in the stillness of my own heart. I longed to be satisfied with the never-letting-go love of God. The truth of God's word resonated and his promise to satisfy came to fruition: "For I will satisfy the weary soul, and every languishing soul I will replenish" (Jer 31:25).

It was enough for me, as I pondered those words that morning, to know that God loved me unconditionally in Christ. It gave me great encouragement, peace, and motivation to be poured out for those whom God had called me to serve. In fact, *as* I was poured out for others that day, I came to appreciate all the more the words that God spoke to the prophet Isaiah:

> If you pour yourself out for the hungry and satisfy the desire of the afflicted, then shall your light rise in the darkness and your gloom be as the noonday. And the LORD will guide you continually and satisfy your desire in scorched places and make your bones strong; and you shall be like a watered garden, like a spring of water, whose waters do not fail. (Isa 58:10–11)

But, as often happens, I forget about the steadfast love of God and my contentment in him fades. This is one of the reasons why we *need* Lord's Day worship each week. In worship, we not only reflect back to God his great worth, but he meets with us in his Word, prayer, and sacraments to *remind* us of his covenant, faithful love. Acknowledging God as he truly is—holy, majestic, sovereign, and faithfully loving— causes us to have a right fear of him. And a right fear of him leads us to rest satisfied in him: "The fear of the LORD leads to life, and whoever has it rests satisfied" (Prov 19:23).

Being satisfied in God, then, means believing that he alone is sufficient for us and that he will meet all of our needs, physically and spiritually. It is trusting in the sovereign love of God, knowing that all things work together for good for those who love God and are called according to his purpose. It is boasting in the strength and merits of Christ on our behalf, knowing that he has accomplished for us everything that God has required of us. Being satisfied in God is being content in whatever circumstances befall us—in plenty or in want, in sickness or in health—because God is our greatest treasure.

Learning Contentment in Suffering

In the passage that we have been following through the course of this book, Paul speaks of a variety of hardships and sufferings (2 Cor 12:10). But before we look at those, it is important to note that Paul precedes his statement about his contentment with "For the sake of Christ." Because Jesus was Paul's greatest treasure—because Jesus was the life-giving, soul-saving, joy-imparting, and strength-enabling Lord of his life—Paul could be content in any and all circumstances, including those that brought about great suffering and hardship.

The four sufferings Paul mentions are: insults, hardships, persecutions, and calamities. *Insults* are those words and actions that belittle you or poke fun at who you are or what you've done. *Hardships* are those personal sufferings usually brought about by the loss of life, health, income, or possessions. *Persecutions* are those actions by others who seek to inflict harm on you because of your association with and witness for Christ. *Calamities* are brought about by your part in large-scale disasters of nature, nation, war, epidemic, famine, and the like.

Together, these four categories sum up the sufferings one could experience in this earthly life. Paul is arguing from the greater to the lesser—if he can be content in these sufferings, then he can be content in *anything*. What a lesson for us who lack contentment waiting in a fast-food drive through line!

A second point we need to consider is that we should be diligent to *prepare* ourselves to be content in suffering. It's not enough to wait for suffering to come upon us and then hope we respond in faith and obedience. No, we are also called to prepare ourselves beforehand for such events and circumstances. It would do us well to read good literature on this subject, such as *Preparations for Sufferings: Or, the Best Work in the Worst Times* by John Flavel (1630–1691).

We also find this expression of preparation by the prophet Habakkuk who prophesies about the impending Babylonian invasion of Judah. In the final few verses of the book, however, Habakkuk writes:

> Though the fig tree should not blossom, nor fruit be on the vines, the produce of the olive fail and the fields yield no food, the flock be cut off from the fold and there be no herd in the stalls, yet I will rejoice in the LORD; I will take joy in the God of my salvation. *God, the Lord,*

is my strength; he makes my feet like the deer's;
he makes me tread on my high places. (Hab
3:17–19, emphasis mine)

Habakkuk resolves to trust in the Lord, to take joy in
him, and to recognize that God was his strength.

A similar expression is found in Psalm 73:26, where
the psalmist writes, "My flesh and my heart may fail, but
God is the strength of my heart and my portion forever."
May you have a similar resolve: When your heart and health
and family and job and money fail, God will remain your
strength. He becomes strong on your behalf so that you can
say, with Paul, "For when I am weak, then I am strong" (2
Cor 12:10).

Learning contentment in suffering, therefore takes
preparation and a heart that seeks to believe God as the all-
satisfying treasure that he is.

Where is Your Treasure?

Let's get specific for a moment about your treasure. If you
remember from the beginning of this chapter, we looked
at what Jesus said in his Sermon on the Mount: "For where
your treasure is, there your heart will be also" (Matt 6:21).
Your treasure is something that you value, love, and cher-
ish. Most of the time, our treasures are *good things*—family,
jobs, or even church. But it is these things that can most
easily become greater treasures than God. In other words,
we elevate God's good gifts above the Giver and make his
gifts idols.

Let me ask the question this way: What possession,
accolade, gift, degree, or family member—*if lost, killed, or
destroyed*—would cause you to be discontent or to doubt
the love of God?

The writer of Hebrews exhorts us: "Keep your life free from the love of money, and be content with what you have, for he has said, 'I will never leave you nor forsake you'" (Heb 13:5). If we love money (or any created thing) more than God, we will never be truly content.

Thomas Watson gives some valuable insight here: "The comfort of life does not consist in having much." He adds, "How fantastic are some who pine away in discontent for the want of those things which, if they had them, would but render them more ridiculous!"[3] Put simply, treasuring God supplies contentment; treasuring anything else more than God supplies discontentment, discouragement, and disillusionment.

Being Content in the Sovereignty of God

Before we conclude this chapter, we need to remind ourselves—in this study of contentment—that God is sovereign over all things that come to pass. The sovereignty of God is one of God's attributes that speak of his complete control over all things, all people, and all time. Nothing happens apart from his providential governing, not even the death of a sparrow (Matt 10:29).

Because God is sovereign, wise, and works all things for our good and his glory, and if he sees fit to give us many earthly possessions or very little earthly possessions, we can rest in the knowledge that he is in control. Whether we find ourselves in plenty or in want, the sovereignty of God should comfort us, humble us, and grant us a steady contentment in the outworking of his eternal plan.

When we are weak in *sin* or in *circumstance*, we can find satisfied contentment in the steadfast love of the Lord.

3. Watson, *Art of Divine Contentment*, 26, 30.

We can find hope that God will never leave us nor forsake us. We can find encouragement that God is sovereign over all and that all things come to pass according to his infinitely wise and sovereign purpose. And we find strength in knowing that nothing will separate us from the love of God in Christ Jesus. When we find ourselves weakened by sin or circumstance, we can find strength in the One who remains strong, faithful, and true on our behalf.

Discussion Questions

- What is the relationship between contentment and godliness?

- What is one way to "learn" contentment?

- Of the list of verses from the Psalms on being satisfied in God, which one or two strikes you as particularly impactful. Why?

- What does it mean to be satisfied in the steadfast love of God?

- What are the four "sufferings" Paul mentions in 2 Corinthians 12:10? How do these four summarize the various sufferings we experience in this life?

- Why is it important to *prepare* for suffering?

- How does a greater understanding of the sovereignty of God encourage you to be content?

9

Leading Others by Losing Yourself

Do you ever take the initiative? If you do, you're a leader. Leaders take initiative. Most leadership books and seminars today will tell you to highlight your talents and downplay your weaknesses. But does this kind of leadership point to the sufficiency and strength of God on your behalf?

As you might imagine from the content of this book and from the present chapter title, I would like to take what we have examined in the previous chapters and present a biblical pattern of leadership that emphasizes, not strengths, but weaknesses—while using your God-given spiritual gifts for his glory and the good of others. You don't have to have an official "leader" role to incorporate the principles set forth in this chapter, just a desire to initiate a pattern of living that highlights the strength of Christ on your behalf.

In this chapter, we will examine three principles of leading—utilizing your weaknesses for God's glory and your joy. Ultimately, what we will see is a biblical pattern for *servant* leadership and *dependent* leadership.

Principle 1: Leading with Intent

Leading through brokenness doesn't come *naturally*. By nature, we want to lead with our strengths because it makes us look good and the attention is directed our way. Obviously, the reason we want attention directed our way is so that we might be accepted and loved. But when the gospel meets us at this most basic of human needs (love and acceptance), it radically shapes our perception of leading others. What does this kind of leading—one that has in view God's grace and sovereign love—look like?

Paul, as a leader in the Christian church, was thankful for the spiritual gifts and offices that he had received—preacher, teacher, apostle, etc. But he also spoke about his sin and weakness so that he became merely a pointer to the One who saved him and gave him those gifts. Leading through brokenness magnifies God and, as we will see, brings great freedom and joy.

Because leading through brokenness and out of weakness doesn't come naturally, we must be intentional with such a model of leading. Our intent should be singular upon bringing glory to God by savoring him as the all-satisfying treasure that he is. Because of our sin, we must work hard to diligently pursue those means by which God sharpens and molds our intent. Practically speaking, what are some of these means?

The primary means that God has given his church to save and sanctify her, and to mold her intentions and affections after him, are his Word, prayer, and the sacraments of baptism and the Lord's Supper. These take place in the context of the local church community, which should be marked by gospel grace. Leading with brokenness cannot happen apart from regularly and diligently availing oneself to these "means of grace." These means, then, form the soil out of which God grows his people and shapes their motivation to lead others.

Principle 2: Leading in Community

While Christianity is personal, it isn't private. The "me-and-Jesus" syndrome that has plagued America is tearing the very fiber of what it means to be the church or the "body" of Christ (cf. 1 Cor 12:12–31). God has ordained, in his wise governing, to save and sanctify a people from every nation and tribe and language so that we might truly experience life *together*.

This covenant community—the church universal—has been elected before the foundations of the earth were laid, bought by the precious blood of Christ, and sealed by the Spirit until the day of Christ. This communion of saints is a community of sinner-saints. They are sinful—more than they could imagine—but called "holy" by God. In fact, Paul often called the recipients of his letters, "saints," which literally means *holy ones*.

When you lead in the Christian community, you are called to recognize your divine call in view of God's mercy. We always are to keep an eye to the grace and mercy of God in our own lives as we lead others around us. As one pastor has said, "You will never outgrow your need for the gospel." You never move on past the gospel after you're saved. It continues to train you in gospel sanctification.

When I was younger, my mom used to tell me to put on my "Sunday best" as we prepared ourselves for Lord's Day worship. While I understand the concept and think it can be a healthy practice, over the years, I have seen a negative side effect to the idea of our Sunday best. We often spend much more time preparing our outfits and looks than we do in preparing our heart for worship. Looking like we have it all together *can lead* to the (unintended) belief that we *do* have it all together.

But the worship that God accepts is a broken and contrite heart (cf. Ps 51:17) in response to his grace and mercy. We come to worship not primarily as givers, but as receivers. We come into his presence to engage in holy dialogue, to be instructed by his Word, to be nourished at his table, and to be sent out in the strength of Christ.

In no way should we come into the communion of saints in worship with a sense of self-righteous boasting, self-exalting gifts, or self-directed praise. As we lead others by losing ourselves, we should strive to express the fact that we are simply beggars showing other beggars where to find the Bread of life.

Principle 3: Leading in Your Home and at Your Job

Oddly enough, two of the most difficult places for people to lead through brokenness are in the home and at the job. Because we are not very good at keeping short accounts with our spouse and children—and because they know the good, the bad, and the ugly about us—boasting in weaknesses and modeling brokenness in the home takes an extra measure of humility. It's difficult when you are short with your wife and then boast in the weakness of being short with your wife. Likewise, it is difficult when your husband or child says something cutting against you and for you to say, "You're right . . . and that's not the worst of it!"

Similarly, leading through brokenness at your job seems like the opposite of what might be expected. However, I've found that those employees who are humble and self-deprecating often get along much better with their employers than those who are always trying to one-up their bosses.

Whether it's in the home or at the job, leading through weakness nevertheless highlights your dependence upon divine grace. It emphasizes and expresses the reality that you are secure enough in who you are and whose you are. There is no more condemnation for you and you are God's adopted child, loved and accepted in Christ. That's your true identity, and gladly boasting in weaknesses communicates that precious reality.

Boasting in weakness with your family and at your job takes great courage. For one, you run the risk of ridicule, which might put a damper on your pride or feelings of acceptance. But, maybe that's the lesson to learn! When you boast in weakness, you win either way. More often than not, when I have gone out on a limb to boast in a weakness of mine, the one to whom I have shared *also* opens up. The walls come down and true intimacy is established. And isn't that what we need more and more in the home anyway?

Resting in your God-given identity gives you the motivation and the courage to boast in weakness and boast in Christ's strength on your behalf.

The greatest model of humility and servant leadership, of course, is Jesus Christ. The eternal and majestic Son of God, the second person of the Trinity, stepped down into our world of sin, death, and shame to defeat them all. He came, not to be served, but to serve and to give his life as a ransom for many (Mark 10:45). If you are going to take initiative and lead others, it is absolutely crucial that you follow *the* leader, Jesus Christ.

I close with two stanzas from the old hymn, "When I Survey the Wondrous Cross." May we count our richest gain as loss compared to the surpassing greatness of knowing Christ Jesus our Lord.

When I survey the wondrous cross
On which the Prince of glory died,
My richest gain I count but loss,
And pour contempt on all my pride.

Forbid it, Lord, that I should boast,
Save in the death of Christ my God!
All the vain things that charm me most,
I sacrifice them to His blood.

Discussion Questions

- Why doesn't leading through brokenness come naturally?

- What are the primary means God has provided to grow his church?

- How are we to come to God in worship?

- Have you found it difficult to boast in weakness with your family? Why or why not?

- Have you found it difficult to boast in weakness at your job? Why or why not?

- Where does the motivation and courage to boast in weakness come from?

Bibliography

Bennett, Arthur, ed. *The Valley of Vision: A Collection of Puritan Prayers and Devotions*. Edinburgh: Banner of Truth Trust, 1975.

Bray, Gerald, ed. *Galatians, Ephesians*. Reformation Commentary on Scripture. Edited by Timothy George and Scott M. Manetsch. Downers Grove: IVP Academic, 2011.

Calvin, John. *Calvin's Bible Commentaries: Corinthians, Part 2*. Translated by John King. Charleston, SC: Forgotten Books, 2007.

Chapell, Bryan. *Holiness By Grace: Delighting in the Joy that is Our Strength*. Wheaton: Crossway Books, 2001.

Cosby, Brian. *Suffering and Sovereignty: John Flavel and the Puritans on Afflictive Providence* (Grand Rapids: Reformation Heritage Books, forthcoming 2012).

Elliot, Elisabeth. *Shadow of the Almighty: The Life and Testament of Jim Elliot*. New York: HarperCollins, 1989.

Hart, D. G., and John Muether. *With Reverence and Awe: Returning to the Basics of Reformed Worship*. Phillipsburg, NJ: P & R Publishing, 2002.

Horton, Michael. *The Gospel-Driven Life: Being Good News People in a Bad News World*. Grand Rapids: Baker Books, 2009.

Mahaney, C. J. *Humility: True Greatness*. Sisters, OR: Multnomah Books, 2005.

Munson, James. "8 Snares Set by Fear of Man." June 8, 2010. No pages. Online: http://theresurgence.com/2010/06/08/8-snares-set-by-fear-of-man.

Peck, M. Scott. *The Road Less Traveled: A New Psychology of Love, Traditional Values and Spiritual Growth*. New York: Simon & Schuster, 1978.

Piper, John. "Christ's Power is Made Perfect in Weakness." Sermon preached on July 14, 1991. No Pages. Online: http://www.desiringgod.org/resource-library/sermons/christs-power-is-made-perfect-in-weakness.

Bibliography

Stott, John. *The Cross of Christ*. Downers Grove: InterVarsity Press, 1986.

Thune, Bob, and Will Walker. *The Gospel-Centered Life: A Nine-Lesson Study*. Jenkintown, PA: World Harvest Mission, 2009.

Watson, Thomas. *The Art of Divine Contentment*. Grand Rapids: Soli Deo Gloria Publications, 2001.

Westminster Assembly. *The Westminster Larger Catechism*. 3rd ed. Lawrenceville, GA: Committee for Christian Education & Publications, 1990.

Zacharias, Ravi. "Our Disappointments Matter to God." Ravi Zacharias International Ministries. No Pages. Online: http://www.rzim.org/justthinkingfv/tabid/602/articleid/76/cbmoduleid/881/default.aspx.